Gospel Evidences of Saving Faith

SERIES EDITORS

Joel R. Beeke & Jay T. Collier

Interest in the Puritans continues to grow, but many people find the reading of these giants of the faith a bit unnerving. This series seeks to overcome that barrier by presenting Puritan books that are convenient in size and unintimidating in length. Each book is carefully edited with modern readers in mind, smoothing out difficult language of a bygone era while retaining the meaning of the original authors. Books for the series are thoughtfully selected to provide some of the best counsel on important subjects that people continue to wrestle with today.

Gospel Evidences of Saving Faith

John Owen

Edited by
Brian G. Hedges

Reformation Heritage Books
Grand Rapids, Michigan

Gospel Evidences of Saving Faith

Reformation Heritage Books
2965 Leonard St. NE
Grand Rapids, MI 49525
616-977-0889 / Fax 616-285-3246
orders@heritagebooks.org
www.heritagebooks.org

Originally published as *Gospel Grounds and Evidences of the Faith of God's Elect* (London, 1695).

Printed in the United States of America
16 17 18 19 20 21/10 9 8 7 6 5 4 3 2 1

Library of Congress Cataloging-in-Publication Data

Names: Owen, John, 1616-1683, author. | Hedges, Brian G., editor.
Title: Gospel evidences of saving faith / John Owen ; edited by Brian G. Hedges.
Other titles: Gospel grounds and evidences of the faith of God's elect
Description: Grand Rapids, Michigan : Reformation Heritage Books, 2016. | Series: Puritan treasures for today | Originally published as: Gospel grounds and evidences of the faith of God's elect. 1695.
Identifiers: LCCN 2016014473 (print) | LCCN 2016016236 (ebook) | ISBN 9781601784612 (pbk. : alk. paper) | ISBN 9781601784629 (epub)
Subjects: LCSH: Faith.
Classification: LCC BT771.3 .O94 2016 (print) | LCC BT771.3 (ebook) | DDC 234—dc23
LC record available at https://lccn.loc.gov/2016014473

Table of Contents

Preface

John Owen was born in 1616, the same year that William Shakespeare died. While Shakespeare is justly famous as the greatest playwright in the history of the English language, Owen is arguably our greatest theologian. The son of a minister himself, Owen lived through both the highest and lowest points of the Puritan era. He served as Oliver Cromwell's chaplain in the 1650s. He opposed the move to make Cromwell king in 1657. And after the restoration of the monarchy in 1660, he faced persecution for being a nonconformist, which significantly curtailed his influence and changed the course of the rest of his life and ministry.

Though he was raised in a Puritan household, Owen did not come to a settled assurance concerning his own salvation until 1642. He attended a church service at St. Mary Aldermanbury, London, and expected to hear the famous Edmund Calamy preach. But a substitute, whose name Owen never discovered, filled the pulpit instead and preached from the text "Why are ye fearful, O ye of little faith?" (Matt. 8:26) God used this sermon to bring Owen to assurance of his salvation.[1]

Owen published his first book the next year, beginning a writing career that would span four decades. He wrote more than eighty books, some of which were published after his death. Many of these books have endured as spiritual classics and have been republished in recent decades. These include his well-known trilogy on sin, recently republished as *Overcoming Sin and Temptation;* his substantial defense of particular redemption in *The Death of Death in the Death of Christ;* his devotional exposition of Trinitarian spirituality in *Of Communion with God the Father, Son, and Holy Ghost;* his magnificent *Meditations and Discourses on the Glory of Christ;* and his magnum opus, *Pneumatologia: A Discourse Concerning the Holy Spirit. Gospel Evidences of Saving Faith* is one of the lesser-known gems in the vast treasure trove that fills the twenty-four volumes of Owen's collected *Works.*[2]

---

1. For a brief biography of Owen, see the entry in Joel Beeke and Randall J. Pederson, *Meet the Puritans: With a Guide to Modern Reprints* (Grand Rapids: Reformation Heritage Books, 2007), 455–63. For a full-length biography, see Peter Toon, *God's Statesman: The Life and Work of John Owen* (Exeter, England: Paternoster Press, 1971), or Crawford Gribben, *John Owen and English Puritanism: Experiences of Defeat* (Oxford: Oxford University Press, 2016).

2. *The Works of John Owen*, ed. W. H. Goold, 24 vols. (1850–1853; repr., Edinburgh: Banner of Truth, 1966). Subsequent citations of Owen's *Works* are from the Banner of Truth edition. The trilogy on sin is comprised of three books: *Of the Mortification of Sin in Believers; Of Temptation: The Nature and Power of It, Etc.;* and *The Nature, Power, Deceit and Prevalency*

The Value of This Book

Few topics are more vital to vibrant Christian living than faith. The Scriptures teach not only that we are justified by faith (Gal. 2:16), but also that we are sanctified by faith (Acts 26:18), receive the Spirit by hearing with faith (Gal. 3:2, 5, 14), and become children of God by faith (John 1:12–13; Gal. 3:26). The righteous are said to live by faith (Rom. 1:17; Gal. 3:22). Without faith it is impossible to please God (Heb. 11:6). We walk by faith, not by sight (2 Cor. 5:7). We live by faith in the Son of God who loved us and gave Himself for us (Gal. 2:20). And whatever does not proceed from faith is sin (Rom. 14:23). The whole life of the Christian is to be a life of faith.

But sometimes there is great confusion concerning the nature and evidences of genuine faith. We know from Scripture that there is such a thing as dead faith

---

of the Remainders of Indwelling Sin in Believers, all in *Works,* vol. 6. These volumes have been published together as *Overcoming Sin and Temptation,* ed. Justin Taylor and Kelly M. Kapic (Wheaton, Ill.: Crossway, 2006). *The Death of Death in the Death of Christ* is found in *Works,* vol. 10 and has been published separately with an introduction by J. I. Packer by Banner of Truth. *Of Communion with God* is found in *Works,* vol. 2 and has been republished as *Communion with the Triune God,* ed. Justin Taylor and Kelly M. Kapic (Wheaton, Ill.: Crossway, 2007). *Meditations and Discourses on the Glory of Christ* is found in *Works,* vol. 1; and *Pneumatologia: A Discourse Concerning the Holy Spirit,* in *Works,* vols. 3–4. A number of Owen's books have also been published in paperback abridgements and modernizations. The original title of the present work was *Gospel Grounds and Evidences of the Faith of God's Elect.* It is found in *Works,* 5:401–57.

(James 2:14–26). And we have examples in Scripture of some who "believed" but proved, in the end, not to be true disciples of Jesus after all (see, for example, John 2:23–25; 8:31–37). Few things are more important than to understand the essential nature of saving faith, to have the skills by which to discern the evidences of saving faith in our lives, and to know how to exercise our faith so as to thrive spiritually. Rare is the book that accomplishes these pastoral, diagnostic functions while at the same time keeping our eyes steadily fixed on the object of faith—namely, Christ Himself. In this short book originally titled *Gospel Grounds and Evidences of the Faith of God's Elect,* John Owen did both. There are four specific reasons why this book remains valuable to the church today.

First, *Owen highlighted the difference between gospel, or evangelical, Christianity and all other systems of religion.* This difference is not always obvious, especially in books addressed to the practical lives of Christians. Many books (and sermons) abound with moral directions and practical exhortations, yet fail to distinguish gospel Christianity from mere religion.

It is now in vogue to use "gospel" as an adjective. Books on "gospel" holiness or being "gospel centered" or "gospel driven" fill our shelves. Perhaps some readers are even beginning to tire of this trend, viewing it as little more than a passing theological fad. I offer no comment on these titles; my point is only that Owen predated the gospel-centered movement by three and one-half centuries! It is not uncommon to find "gospel" used as an adjective in Owen's works. Indeed, he did so in this book at least nine times, as he wrote six times of "gospel holiness," twice of "gospel repentance," and once each of "gospel graces" and "gospel ordinances."

Then, there is the original title itself, *Gospel Grounds and Evidences of the Faith of God's Elect*. It is possible that the publishers gave it this title rather than Owen himself, as the treatise was not published until 1695, some twelve years after Owen's death. Nevertheless, the title accurately describes the content of Owen's book, as he examined both the grounds and the evidences of saving faith and gave considerable space and effort to distinguishing true saving faith from that which is false. Owen's intended audience, as the historically savvy reader might well guess, included Roman Catholics, Quakers, and Socinians. Owen was deeply concerned with the formalism, superstition, and legalism of Roman Catholicism; the mysticism of the Quakers; and the rationalism of the Socinians. Over and against them all, he maintained that true saving faith was distinctively grounded upon and shaped by the gospel, which he defined as "the divine declaration of the way of God for the saving of sinners, through the person, mediation, blood, righteousness, and intercession of Christ." In Owen's thinking, the very essence and life of faith consist in the soul's discerning and giving hearty consent to

God's way of saving sinners through the Son's work on the cross. True faith consents to this way of salvation as that which both most glorifies God in all of His holy and gracious attributes, and most satisfies and delights the regenerate mind and heart. Where this evangelical conviction is lacking, saving faith is absent.

Driven by this firm conviction, Owen was not content to exhort readers merely to test themselves by external moral, behavioral, or religious practices. Instead, he pressed upon his readers the necessity of a real, inward work of grace in the soul, leading it to renounce all other hopes and means for salvation and so cast itself on God's grace revealed in Christ alone. This, for Owen, was true evangelical Christianity, the full embrace of which is the first evidence of saving faith.

Second, *this naturally leads Owen to demonstrate the true nature of saving faith in a way that avoids the errors of both legalism and antinomianism.* Although Owen did not use the words "legalism" and "antinomianism" in this work, he did show that the truly regenerate person can be distinguished from both "profligate sinners" on one hand, and "those who are under legal convictions" on the other. The difference lies in the regenerate soul's undying desire for God's glory in all things, which inclines the heart to a deep and abiding approval of God's holiness. "The first beam of spiritual light and grace," said Owen, "creates an indefatigable desire for the glory of God in their minds and souls."

It is this desire for God's glory that preserves the believing soul from both the Scylla of legalism and the Charybdis of antinomianism. The believer so deeply desires God's glory that he or she can embrace no way of salvation as suited and fitting for a holy God except the way proposed in the gospel; namely, salvation through the mediatorial work of Jesus Christ. This keeps the soul from legalism—that is, from trusting in his or her moral merits or performance of the law as an adequate ground for acceptance by God. But this same impulse and inclination of the regenerate heart for God's glory also preserves the believer from antinomianism—that is, from dishonoring or disregarding God's law ("antinomian" derives from two Greek words: *anti*, against; *nomos*, law) and thus turning grace into a license for sin. The same spiritual light that creates a desire for God's glory is also "the spring and principle" of gospel holiness.

As Owen demonstrated in the second chapter of his book, the second evidence of genuine faith is precisely this: habitually approving of the holiness and obedience that God requires, both because it honors God, who is holy, and also because it is that for which He created us. We were, after all, originally created in God's image, and it is according to His image that we are now being renewed (Eph. 4:24). Holiness is, therefore, that "which gives...rectitude and perfection to our nature of which it is capable in this world." And true believers, though they may often fall due to the temptations of sin and the weakness of the flesh, are never satisfied with anything less than their ongoing growth in holiness, their continual and progressive transformation into the glorious image of Christ.

Third, *Owen provided practical direction for believers regarding repentance and the pursuit of assurance.* His aim throughout is to show the grounds of saving faith and the chief and primary evidences of it. But his purpose was not to provide a manual by which we could discern these evidences in others as much as to test ourselves.

Owen chose to highlight four evidences, to which the four chapters of the book roughly correspond. The first evidence, as mentioned above, is embracing and approving of God's way of saving sinners through Christ as that which most glorifies God, satisfies our own souls, and honors God's law. I have also already given attention to the second evidence—namely, the approval of the holiness and obedience that God requires.

In the third and shortest chapter of the book, Owen discusses the evidence of "consistently endeavoring to keep all grace in exercise in all ordinances of divine worship, both private and public." By "grace in exercise," Owen means the inward workings of evangelical graces such as faith, hope, and love—what Jonathan Edwards would later call "religious affections."[3] There is a dif-

3. Jonathan Edwards, *Religious Affections,* ed. John E. Smith, in *The Works of Jonathan Edwards,* vol. 2 (New Haven, Conn.: Yale University Press, 1959).

ference between simply going through the motions of prayer and worship and sincerely directing our hearts toward the Father through Spirit-empowered faith in Christ. Owen was concerned with the dangers of formalism and superstition in worship and viewed the internal exercises of grace as the chief preservative against apostasy from genuine gospel worship. His directions are as practical as they are brief. Consistently applied, they will prove helpful to any believer who struggles with formality and coldness of heart in either private devotions or public worship.

But in chapter 4 Owen excels in giving practical advice to the struggling, doubting Christian. For, as the fourth evidence of saving faith, Owen proposed a special state of repentance in which the believing soul could give focused effort to exercise faith and bring the heart into a spiritual frame. Owen took pains to clarify that he did not mean here evangelical repentance, which must characterize all believers (although the repentance he intended is not different in *kind* from gospel repentance). Instead, he meant a particular *degree* of repentance that he deemed necessary for six sorts of people, whom he carefully described. Seven specific ingredients or requirements necessary for this special state of repentance followed. This is Owen at his pastoral best, as he provided seasoned counsel for struggling Christians and urged upon them the necessity of detachment from the world, godly sorrow for sin, mortification of the flesh, watchfulness over their hearts in times of solitude, longing for deliverance, and abounding in spiritual thoughts. This program will prove immensely helpful to any backslidden or doubting believer as well as to pastors and counselors who are trying to help them.

Finally, *Owen excelled in describing and diagnosing the spiritual experience of a believer.* This, of course, is related to the previous point, but it bears special mention. For Owen, like few other physicians of the soul, was able to use the scalpel of God's Holy Word to probe the inner recesses of the saint's thoughts, inclinations, and affections.

Owen was especially skillful in helping believers understand the complexities of their own hearts. He recognized that apparently contradictory thoughts and desires coexist in the hearts of the regenerate. For example, Owen showed that "there is no inconsistency between spiritual joy in Christ and godly sorrow for sin." Indeed, he contended that mourning for sin is necessary to the maintenance of "solid joy" in the heart. "Yes," he wrote, "there is a secret joy and refreshment in godly sorrow, and a great spiritual satisfaction, that is equal to the highest of our joys."

In like manner, Owen demonstrated that the believer is characterized by both "the deepest humiliation" as well as "a refreshing sense of the love of God and peace with him." Again, the true Christian experiences "trouble and anxiety of mind" concerning his sins; but this kind of anxiety "is not…opposed to spiritual peace and refreshment." In fact, as Owen wrote in the final paragraph of his book, it is "those who have the lowest thoughts of themselves, and are most filled with self-abasement" who "have the clearest views of divine glory."

Owen also explained how a believer's faith can evidence itself in the darkness of temptation and sin. After having argued that the second evidence of saving faith is its unwavering approval of the holiness and obedience God requires, Owen showed that faith evidences itself by the "self-dissatisfaction and humiliation, which it stirs up any time the mind falls short of this holiness." Far from leading the true believer into the agony of doubt, Owen showed that genuine faith is the root of "holy shame" for sin. So, even in "the disquieting conflicts" waged by sin "in and against our souls" and the "decays we may fall into…as long as inward holy shame and godly sorrow for sin is preserved, faith is evident in us."

Perhaps the best example of Owen's insight into spiritual experience comes from the first chapter of the book, where he stated that a "soul enlightened with the knowledge of the truth, and made aware of its own condition by spiritual conviction, has two predominant desires, by which it is wholly regulated." The first of those desires is that "God may be glorified." The second, "that the soul itself may be eternally saved." "These desires are inseparable in any enlightened soul," said Owen. This distinguishes the true believer from others.

For unlike the profligate or the religious hypocrite, a regenerate person cannot desire his or her own salvation apart from the desire for God to be glorified. But the gospel—God's way of saving sinners through Jesus Christ—"brings these desires into a perfect consistency and harmony [and] also causes them to increase and promote one another." Owen asserted,

> The desire for God's glory increases the desire for our own salvation; and the desire for our own salvation enlarges and inflames the desire for glorifying God in it. These things are brought into a perfect consistency and mutual usefulness in the blood of Christ.... For this is the way that God, in infinite wisdom, has planned to glorify himself in the salvation of sinners.

Such is the spiritual perception that pervades all of Owen's writings, including this book. When blessed by the Holy Spirit, such observations not only instruct but also help to cultivate in our hearts the spiritual graces of faith, repentance, brokenness, humility, joy, and peace.

A Note on the Editing

Owen is notoriously difficult to read, which is perhaps one reason why this particular book has not been separately published in the last century. In editing this book, my goal has been to preserve the structure and substance of Owen's argument while making it more accessible to modern readers. This has involved replacing many archaic terms with more familiar words. For example, "approbation" has been replaced with "approval," "displicency" with "dissatisfaction," and "disquietment" with "anxiety." But making Owen accessible has also involved simplifying his syntax: breaking long, complex sentences into shorter, simpler ones; changing verbs from the passive to active voice; removing redundancies; clarifying (and occasionally supplying) references to Scripture; and arranging sentence structure so as to best facilitate ready understanding on the part of the reader.

I have also sought to make the overall structure of Owen's work more transparent to the reader. Owen, like many of his contemporaries, could get carried away with numerical points, subpoints, sub-subpoints, and even sub-sub-subpoints. Sometimes it is difficult for even the most attentive reader to know which points go with which! In the case of this book, I have not reordered the argument itself, but I have tried to make the actual structure of the argument more transparent to the reader. I have done this in several ways: by providing a table of contents that shows the basic outline of the book in its main divisions (although not in every digression); by adding numbered division headings into each of the four parts; by smoothing out and, in some cases, slightly expanding Owen's transitions; and, in some places, by replacing pronouns with their antecedents in order to make Owen's points more apparent.

I believe that the final product retains both the substance and tone of Owen's book, making it more accessible to twenty-first-century readers. My hope and prayer is that new readers will discover in Owen the same spiritual nourishment that I have found.

—Brian G. Hedges

Introduction

It is vitally important, for both the glory of God and the advantage of believers through the gospel, that believers obtain spiritual comforts, for God abundantly desires that all the heirs of promise should receive strong consolation, and He has provided ways and means to give this comfort to them. Their share in this comfort is their most basic concern and their highest priority in this world. But the power of remaining sin, along with other temptations, stands in opposition to believers' effective and refreshing enjoyment of these comforts. And so, in spite of their right to enjoy these comforts, believers often lack a gracious sense of them and consequently lack the relief these comforts can provide through all the believer's duties, trials, and afflictions.

True and saving faith—the faith of God's elect—is the root on which all genuine comforts grow. These comforts, therefore, are ordinarily shared by believers in proportion to the evidences of true faith in their lives. Spiritual comforts cannot be maintained without these evidences. Therefore, in order to help believers either establish or recover a sense of these comforts, I will ask, what are the principal acts and operations of faith by which it demonstrates its genuineness in the midst of all temptations and storms that befall believers in this world?

In my answer I will insist on only those evidences that will bear the severest scrutiny by Scripture and experience.

These evidences are as follows:

1. Choosing, embracing, and approving God's way of saving sinners through the work of Christ alone
2. Habitually approving of the holiness and obedience God requires as revealed in Scripture
3. Consistently endeavoring to keep all grace in exercise in all ordinances of divine worship
4. Bringing the soul into a special state of repentance

CHAPTER 1

First Evidence: Choosing, Embracing, and Approving God's Way of Saving Sinners through the Work of Christ Alone

The most basic act of saving faith is choosing, embracing, and approving of God's way of saving sinners by the mediation of Jesus Christ, relying on Him alone, while renouncing all other alleged ways and means of salvation. This is what I will explain and prove.

Saving faith is our *believing the record* "that God gave of his Son" (1 John 5:10). "And this is the record, that God hath given to us eternal life, and this life is in his Son" (v. 11). This is the testimony which God gives, that great and sacred truth which He Himself bears witness unto: namely, that He has freely prepared eternal life for those who believe. He has provided a way of salvation for them. And what God so prepares He is said to *give,* because of the certainty of its bestowal. So God promised and gave grace to the elect in Christ Jesus before the world began (2 Tim. 1:9; Titus 1:2). And this grace is to be given to the elect, in and by the mediation of His Son

Jesus Christ, that it is the only way by which God will give eternal life unto anyone.

Grace is therefore wholly in Christ Jesus: it is obtained by Him and received from Him. Our eternal safety or ruin absolutely depends on our approval of this testimony, upon our approval and praise of this way of saving sinners or our refusal of it. And it is reasonable that it should be so: for, by receiving this testimony of God, we "set to [our] seal that God is true" (John 3:33). This is how we ascribe to Him the glory of His truth and, in this, all His other holy attributes. This is the most prestigious duty of which we are capable in this world. If we refuse this testimony, we make Him a liar (1 John 5:10). This is virtually equivalent to denying His existence altogether.

The solemnity with which this testimony is announced is very remarkable. "There are three that bear record in heaven, the Father, the Word, and the Holy Ghost: and these three are one" (1 John 5:7). The divine Trinity, acting distinctly in the unity of the same divine nature, give this testimony. They do so by their distinct operations of salvation. The gospel declares these divine acts. To this is added a testimony that immediately applies this sovereign testimony of the Holy Trinity to the souls of believers. This is the witness of grace and all sacred ordinances: "There are three that bear witness in earth, the Spirit, and the water, and the blood: and these three agree in one" (1 John 5:8). These are not the same in nature as are the Father, Son, and Holy Ghost, yet they all agree in the same testimony. And they do this by their effectiveness in the souls of believers in assuring them of this truth. Life and death are solemnly and gloriously set before us in this record. Embracing this testimony is the work of faith that secures for us eternal life. Only in these terms is reconciliation established between God and men. Without this, men must forever perish.

So our blessed Savior affirms: "This is life eternal, that they may know thee" (the Father) "the only true God, and Jesus Christ whom thou hast sent" (John 17:3). To know the Father as the only true God, to know Him as He has sent Jesus Christ to be the only way and means saving sinners, and to know Jesus Christ as sent by the Father for this purpose, is that grace and duty that gives us a right to eternal life and gives us possession of it.

Further Explanation of the Nature of Saving Faith

But these things need to be more carefully explained.

1. The way by which sinners may be saved is the fundamental issue that distinguishes religions from one another. Other differences about religion arise from men's varying perceptions of salvation. And the first thing that engages men to be really concerned with religion is this question: How may sinners be saved? What shall we do? What shall we do to be saved? What is

the way of acceptance with God? (see Acts 2:37; 16:30; Mic. 6:6–8).

Once the conscience raises this question, it must have an answer. The prophet says, I will "see...what I shall answer when I am reproved" (Hab. 2:1). And there is all the reason in the world why men should consider a good answer to this question; without it they will perish forever. For if they cannot answer themselves here, how do they hope to answer God hereafter? Therefore, without a sufficient answer to this question always in hand, no one can have any hopes of a blessed eternity.

The answer people give to themselves is according to the influence of one of the two divine covenants upon their mind: the covenant of works or the covenant of grace. These covenants, taken absolutely, are inconsistent and give answers in this case that directly contradict one another, as the apostle Paul declares in Romans 10:5–9. The one says, "*The man that does the works of the law shall live by them*; this is the only way in which you may be saved." The other wholly renounces this answer and places all *faith in Christ Jesus*. Thus there is a great difference in the answers men give to themselves on this inquiry, for their consciences will only speak and hear that which agrees with the covenant to which they belong. These things are reconciled only in the blood of Christ (Rom. 8:3). The majority of convicted sinners seem to adhere to the testimony of the covenant of works—and so perish forever. Nothing will save us, though, "but the answer of a good conscience toward God...by the resurrection of Jesus Christ" (1 Peter 3:21).

2. The way God has prepared for the saving of sinners is the fruit of infinite wisdom. It is powerful and effectual in accomplishing its purpose. As such it must be either received or rejected. But it is not enough to simply agree with the concept. We must also perceive the divine wisdom and power of this way in order to safely entrust ourselves to it. Some look upon God's way of salvation and embrace it as the power and wisdom of God. Others reject it as foolish and weak, not worthy of being trusted. This difference results in an eternally distinguishing difference among men. Paul describes this difference in 1 Corinthians 1:18–24. It is mysterious that the same divine truth is, by the same way and means, at the same time, proposed unto different persons, all in the same condition, under the same circumstances, all equally concerned in that which is proposed in the truth, yet received entirely differently. Some receive the truth, embrace it, approve of it, and trust themselves to it for life and salvation. Others despise it, reject it, do not value it, and do not trust themselves to it. To the one it is *the wisdom* of God, and *the power* of God; to the other, *weakness and foolishness.* And it must necessarily be one or the other—there is no middle consideration. It is not a good way unless it is the only way. It is not a safe way if it is not the best way, or

if there is any other way, for this way is eternally inconsistent with any other. It is the wisdom of God, or it is downright folly. Only eternal sovereign grace makes the distinction between those who are given the gospel, and the almighty power of actual grace in curing the unbelief that blinds the minds of men, so that they see only folly and weakness in God's way of saving sinners. This unbelief still works in the majority of those to whom the gospel has proposed God's way of salvation. They do not receive it as a result of infinite wisdom, nor as powerful and effectual to salvation. Some recklessly feed their lusts and disregard the gospel. To others the words of the prophet apply, "Behold, ye despisers, and wonder, and perish" (Acts 13:41, quoting Hab. 1:5). Some are under the power of darkness and ignorance; they do not comprehend the mystery of the gospel: "The light shineth in darkness; and the darkness comprehended it not" (John 1:5). Satan, the god of this world, has blinded some, filling their minds with prejudice and their hearts with the love of present things, so that the light of the glorious gospel of Christ, who is the image of God, cannot shine into them. Some mix the gospel with their own works, ways, and duties, which belong to the covenant of works and which are eternally irreconcilable unto God's way of salvation (Rom. 10:3–4). This is how unbelief eternally ruins the souls of men. They do not, they cannot, approve of God's plan of salvation as the gospel proposes it. They do not see it as an effect of infinite wisdom and power, to which they could safely entrust themselves in opposition to all other ways and means that allegedly bring salvation. Understanding this will give us light into the nature and actions of saving faith.

3. The whole Scripture, and all divine institutions from the beginning, testify that God's way of salvation for sinners is by an exchange, substitution, atonement, satisfaction, and imputation. This is the language of the first promise and all the sacrifices of the law that are founded on it. The Scriptures teach that there is a way whereby sinners may be saved, a way that God has appointed. Now, since the law is concerned with sinners, we might expect their relationship to God to be wholly determined by what they can do or suffer in respect to the law. "No," says the Scripture, "it cannot be so; for 'by the deeds of the law there shall no flesh be justified in [God's] sight'" (Rom. 3:20; also see Ps. 143:2; Gal. 2:16). Neither shall they save themselves by paying the penalty of the law that they have broken. For they cannot, but must perish eternally: for, "if thou, LORD, shouldest mark iniquities, O Lord, who shall stand?" (Ps. 130:3). There must be another way of salvation that is of a different nature. If not, then Scripture's revelation of God's mind is inadequate and misleading. But the main purpose of Scripture is to declare that there is another way: the substitution of a mediator in place of the sinners. This mediator shall bear the penalty of the law incurred

by those sinners and fulfill the righteousness which they could not attain.

This is God's way of saving sinners, whether men like it or not. Romans 8 explains,

> For what the law could not do, in that it was weak through the flesh, God sending his own Son in the likeness of sinful flesh, and for sin, condemned sin in the flesh: that the righteousness of the law might be fulfilled in us, who walk not after the flesh, but after the Spirit. (vv. 3–4; see also Heb. 10:5–10)

In 2 Corinthians, Paul writes, "For he hath made him to be sin for us, who knew no sin; that we might be made the righteousness of God in him" (5:21).

Unbelief has prevailed upon many in our time to reject God's glory, revealed in the gospel, but we have vindicated the truth against them sufficiently elsewhere.[1]

4. There are several prerequisites to having a clear view of God's glory in, and as a result of, His plan of salvation. These are a due consideration of the nature of the fall of our first parents and our resulting apostasy from God. I will not stop here to discuss all of the nature and implications of the fall, for we cannot fully understand

---

1. See especially John Owen, *Vindiciae Evangelicae; or, The Mystery of the Gospel Vindicated and Socinianism Examined*, in *The Works of John Owen*, ed. W. H. Goold (Edinburgh: Banner of Truth, 1966), 12:1–616.

them, much less express them. I will only say this: unless we have due apprehensions of the dread and terror of the fall and apostasy of our first parents, of the invasion sin made on the glory of God, and of the confusion the fall brought upon creation, we will never see why rejecting the way of personal righteousness and embracing mediatorial salvation is both reasonable and glorious. A right sense of our infinite distance from God and the impossibility of our approaching Him is of the same consideration. We must also consider man's inability to do anything that may satisfy the law, or the holiness and righteousness of God in the law; that is, our universal lack of conformity in our natures, hearts, and their actions to the nature, holiness, and will of God. Unless we have a sense of these things in our minds and on our consciences, we cannot believe rightly or comprehend the glory of this new way of salvation. Mankind has had a general notion, though not a clear understanding, of these things (or of some of them); many people have grasped that some kind of satisfaction or atonement is necessary in order for sinners to be freed from God's displeasure. But when God's way of salvation is proposed to them, they reject it because "the carnal mind is enmity against God" (Rom. 8:7). When sharp and lasting convictions fix these things on the soul, however, they will enlighten it with a true perception of the glory and beauty of God's way of saving sinners.

5. The gospel is a divine declaration of the way of salvation through the person, mediation, blood, righteousness, and intercession of Christ. The gospel reveals, declares, and offers a way of salvation to sinners, if they will only believe. As this is contained in the first promise, so the truth of every word in the Scripture depends upon it. Without this there could be no more fellowship between God and us than there is between God and devils. The gospel declares that this way is not by the law or its works (that is, by the first covenant or its conditions, or by our own doing or suffering), but it is a new way, discovered in and proceeding from infinite wisdom, love, grace, and goodness. This way is through the incarnation of the eternal Son of God, His assuming the office of a mediator, and His doing and suffering as mediator whatever was needful for the justification and salvation of sinners, unto His own eternal glory (see Rom. 3:24–27; 8:3–4; 2 Cor. 5:19–21).

The gospel also says that the only way of obtaining an interest in this blessed plan of salvation through Christ's substitution (the surety of the covenant), the imputation of our sins to Him, and of His righteousness unto us, is *through faith in Christ.*

This is the test of faith after which we inquire. Salvation being proposed, offered, and tendered in the gospel, true and saving faith receives it, approves of it, and rests in it. Saving faith renounces all other hopes and expectations and rests all of its confidence in this way of salvation through Christ alone, for God does not present this way of salvation to us merely as a notion of truth to be assented to or denied (in which case anyone who merely assented to the historical facts of Scripture would be counted a true Christian). No, this way of salvation must be practically embraced. That is, we are to personally entrust ourselves to Christ alone for life and salvation. Therefore, I shall discuss how saving faith approves of this way of salvation and manifests itself to the comfort of believers.

Saving Faith Approves of God's Way of Salvation as That Which Most Glorifies God

How, then, does saving faith approve of God's way of salvation? On what basis and to what end? First, faith approves of this way as fitting for God to plan and give. Paul notes this in Hebrews 2:10: "For it became him, for whom are all things, and by whom are all things, in bringing many sons unto glory, to make the captain of their salvation perfect through sufferings." Only that which corresponds to God's infinite wisdom, goodness, grace, holiness, and righteousness is worthy of God. And this is what faith discerns and approves concerning the way of salvation: that it is worthy of God in every way. It answers every aspect of His holy being. That is why Paul calls salvation "the light of the knowledge of the glory of God in the face of Jesus Christ" (2 Cor. 4:6).

This discovery of the glory of God in this way of salvation is made by faith alone, and by faith alone is it embraced. The unbelief that ruins men's souls is the failure to discern and therefore assent to God's glory in this way of salvation. The reason men do not embrace the way of salvation offered in the gospel is that they do not see nor understand how full it is of divine glory. They do not see how it becomes God, is worthy of Him, and reflects all the perfections of His nature. They are so blinded, that the light of the glorious gospel of Christ, who is the image of God, does not illuminate their minds (2 Cor. 4:4). And so they deal with God's way of salvation as if it were weakness and folly.

The *essence* and *life* of faith consist in this: it sees, discerns, and determines that the way of salvation of sinners by Jesus Christ proposed in the gospel suits God and all His divine attributes. In this, faith thoroughly gives glory to God. This is faith's distinctive work and outstanding feature (Rom. 4:20). In this faith rests and refreshes itself.

Faith in particular rejoices in God's infinite wisdom, manifested in this way of salvation. A view of God's wisdom displayed through His power in the works of creation is sole reason for ascribing glory to God in all natural worship, by which we glorify Him as God. And a due grasp of God's infinite wisdom in the new creation, in the way of saving sinners by Jesus Christ, is the foundation of all spiritual, evangelical worship, by which we ascribe glory to God.

It was God's design, in a special way, to manifest and glorify His wisdom in salvation. Christ crucified is the "power of God, and the wisdom of God" (1 Cor. 1:24). In Him "are hid all the treasures of wisdom and knowledge" (Col. 2:3). All the treasures of divine wisdom are stored and displayed in Christ in order to be manifested to faith in and by the gospel. This is how God designed to make known His "manifold wisdom" (Eph. 3:9–10).

Therefore, according to our comprehension and admiration of God's wisdom in constituting this way of salvation, so is our faith. There is no faith at all if this does not appear to us and if our minds are not affected with it.

I cannot take time here to count the special instances of divine wisdom in this way of salvation, though I have attempted something toward this in other writings.[2] I shall say only that the foundation of salvation, the incarnation of the Son of God, is such a glorious effect of infinite wisdom that the whole blessed creation will eternally admire it. The incarnation in itself indicates that this way and work is divine—in it

2. John Owen, *Christologia: Or, A Declaration of the Glorious Mystery of the Person of Christ—God and Man*, in *The Works of John Owen*, ed. W. H. Goold (Edinburgh: Banner of Truth, 1966), 1:178–223.

the glory of God shines in the face of Jesus Christ. This is of God alone. It is this that becomes Him. Nothing but divine wisdom could extend unto this. Faith is safe as long as it lives in the understanding and grasp of God's wisdom in this foundation and everything that is built upon it.

Salvation also gloriously and richly reveals other properties of God's nature: His goodness, love, grace, and mercy. "God is love" (1 John 4:8). There is no God but the God who is love. Grace and mercy are among the principal titles that God assumes to Himself. It was His aim to manifest all these attributes to the utmost in this work and way of saving sinners by Christ, as is declared throughout Scripture. Scripture lays these attributes open to the eye of faith. Faith sees that such infinite goodness, love, and grace become God and that they can reside in no one but Him. Faith rests and rejoices in this (1 Peter 1:8), and it is in adhering to and approving of this way of salvation as an expression of God's perfections that faith continually acts.

Where unbelief prevails, the mind has no view of God's glory, yet this, too, befits God's character in this way of salvation. The apostle Paul declares it in 2 Corinthians 4:4. And where there is no view of God's glory, men cannot gladly receive and embrace the gospel, whatever they may pretend. For they do not know the reason why they should. They do not see the loveliness of Christ, who is the life and center of this way. They see "no beauty that we should desire him" (Isa. 53:2). It was for this reason that the first preaching of the gospel was a stumbling block to Jews and foolishness to the Greeks. Because of their unbelief, they could not see the gospel as the "the power of God and the wisdom of God." And so must this way of salvation be esteemed, or else counted as folly (1 Cor. 1:23–24).

Yes, it is from the same principle of unbelief that many reject the truth of the gospel, especially those who reject the divinity of Christ and all who disbelieve supernatural mysteries. They cannot see worth in salvation unto the glory of God—no unbeliever can. Therefore neither can those who, though they may not directly oppose the doctrine of the gospel, fail to properly exercise it. Very few, comparatively speaking, who profess the truth of the gospel have an experience of its *power* unto their salvation.

But here, true faith invincibly stands. As long as the soul can exercise its faith in choosing, embracing, and approving of God's way of saving sinners by Jesus Christ and recognize that God works in this way for His own glory and because it is in accordance with His nature, the soul will have sufficient help in all its trials. As long as it can do these things, it may evidence its truth and sincerity in the midst of all temptations and the most dismal conflicts with sin. Yes, such a faith will prevail even against the perplexing power and charge of sin arising from within. Faith will not be driven from this stronghold. For this is faith, saving faith, which will not fail us. This faith graciously persuades the believer's soul of salvation's excellence by revealing the glory of God's wisdom, power, grace, love, and goodness in it. It satisfies the soul with this salvation, the best and only way of coming to God. This faith renounces all other ways and means of salvation, and such a faith will continually prove its sincerity.

This soul gains assurance of its entry into glory upon its departure out of this world. It is a great thing to fully grasp that a poor soul, guilty of many sins, may, when leaving the body (perhaps under great pain, distress, anguish, or even outward violence), immediately be received into God's glorious presence, along with all the holy attendants of His throne, to enjoy eternal rest and blessedness. Here, as well, faith discerns and approves of this great, ineffable, divine operation as that which best suits the infinite greatness of God's wisdom and grace in designing it, the glorious efficacy of Christ's mediation, and the excellence of the Holy Spirit's sanctifying work. Faith approves of this without looking to anything worthy in itself to gain entrance to glory. And no man knows what this glory is or desires it in a right manner if he imagines any correlation between this glory and who he is or what he has done in this world. This is why some who have this faith have invented *purgatory*, a place for making them fit for heaven after having left this world. They do understand the grounds upon which a man should expect an entrance into glory upon his death.

Let them who are exercised with temptations and dejections bring their faith to this trial. And this is the case, in various degrees of us all. First, then, examine strictly by the Word whether this is a true description of the nature and outworking of saving faith. This description assumes or asserts several things: (1) salvation through Jesus Christ is the primary effect of divine wisdom, power, goodness, love, and grace; (2) the purpose of the gospel is to display, declare, and testify to this and make known the glory of God in it; (3) saving faith is that act, duty, and work of the soul by which we receive God's Word concerning these things and ascribe Him the glory for all of them; and (4) the soul renounces all other ways and hopes for acceptance by God, in life and salvation, on this basis, whether these other ways stand in opposition to God's way of salvation or are seen as additions to it.

Examine these four principles strictly by the Word, and if they appear to be (as they are) sacred, evangelical, fundamental truths, do not be moved away from them. Do not be shaken in them by any temptation whatever. Then, test your faith by these principles: What do you believe concerning God's way of saving sinners by Jesus Christ, as proposed in the gospel? Are you satisfied in it as that which is fitting to God and answers all the glorious attributes of His nature? Would you have any other way proposed in its place? Can you, will you, commit the eternal welfare of your souls to the grace and faithfulness of God and desire no other way of salvation? Does God's glory in any measure shine to you in the face of Jesus Christ? Do you find a secret joy in your heart upon the satisfaction you take in the gospel's proposal of this way of salvation? Do you, in all your fears and temptations and in all approaches of death, renounce all other provisions and solaces, and place your whole confidence in this way alone, and the representation of God that it depicts? Here lies faith and its exercise, which will be an anchor to your soul in all its trials.

This is the first and primary reason saving faith accepts, embraces, and approves of God's way of salvation through Christ: because this way is in accordance with each of His holy attributes, which are manifested and glorified in it. And where faith approves of this way on this ground and reason, it evidences itself to be truly evangelical, to the support and comfort of those who believe.

Saving Faith Approves of God's Way of Salvation as That Which Most Satisfies Our Souls

The second way that faith approves of this way of salvation is in finding it suited to *the whole design and all the desires of an enlightened soul.*[3] When our Lord Jesus

3. By "enlightened soul," Owen has in mind the regenerate believer who has experienced the illuminating work of the Holy

Christ compared the kingdom of God (which is this way of salvation) to a treasure and a precious pearl, He affirmed that those who found them had great joy and the highest satisfaction, as having attained that which suited their desires and gave their minds rest. A soul enlightened with the knowledge of the truth and made aware of its own condition by spiritual conviction has two predominant desires by which it is wholly regulated. First, that *God may be glorified*; and, second, that *the soul itself may be eternally saved*. Nor can it give up either of these desires. These desires are inseparable in any enlightened soul, which can never cease desiring them to the highest degree. The whole world is unable to rob an enlightened mind of either of these desires. Profligate sinners have no interest in the former desire—that God may be glorified; nor do those who are under legal convictions (from God's law), if they have not yet received spiritual light. They want to be saved, but they are not concerned about the glory of God. The only thing they desire from salvation is freedom from external misery, and they seek it whether God is glorified or not. They have no desire for true salvation.

Spirit. His use of "light" language is rooted in Scripture (e.g., Ps. 119:18; Luke 24:45; 2 Cor. 4:6; Eph. 1:18; 1 Peter 2:9). For Owen's fuller exposition, see especially chapter 4 in *The Causes, Ways, and Means of Understanding the Mind of God*, in *The Works of John Owen*, ed. W. H. Goold (Edinburgh: Banner of Truth, 1966), 4:163–71.

But the first beam of spiritual light and grace creates an indefatigable desire for the glory of God in their minds and souls. Without this the soul does not know how to desire its own salvation. But the enlightened soul only desires a salvation that glorifies God, for without God being glorified, whatever the soul's state should be, it would not be salvation. The exaltation of the glory of God is essential to salvation; it consists in beholding and enjoying that glory. This desire, therefore, is immovably fixed in the mind and soul of every enlightened person; he will not consider any eternal proposal that is inconsistent with it.

But, moreover, in every such person there is a ruling desire for his *own salvation*. It is natural to him, a creature made for eternity. It is inseparable from him, a convicted sinner. And the clearer the light anyone has about the nature of this salvation, the more this desire is heightened and confirmed in him.

The inquiry, then, is how these two prevalent desires may be reconciled and satisfied in the same mind. For, as we are sinners, there seems to be an inconsistency between them. The glory of God, in His justice and holiness, requires that sinners should perish eternally. The law speaks this verdict, and it is in the language of our conscience and in the voice of all our fears. Therefore, for a sinner to desire that God may be glorified is to desire that he himself be damned.

To which of these desires shall the sinner cleave? Shall he cast off all hopes and desires for his own salvation and be content to forever perish? He cannot do this. God does not require it, for He has given the sinner the opposite command. Shall the sinner then desire that God depart with His glory so that, one way or other, his soul may be saved? Shall he disregard what becomes of God's glory? An enlightened mind cannot do this any more than it can cease to desire its own salvation. But in himself, a sinner can find no way to reconcile these two things.

Here, therefore, the glory of salvation represents itself to the faith of every believer. It not only brings these desires into a perfect consistency and harmony but also causes them to increase and promote one another. The desire for God's glory increases the desire for our own salvation, and the desire for our own salvation enlarges and inflames the desire for glorifying God in it. These things are brought into a perfect consistency and mutual usefulness in the blood of Christ (Rom. 3:24–26). For this is the way that God, in infinite wisdom, has planned to glorify Himself in the salvation of sinners. Everything in which the glory of God consists is reconciled to and consistent with the salvation of sinners. Every property of His nature is gloriously exalted in and by it. In this, an answer is given to all the objections of the law against the consistency of God's glory and the salvation of sinners. The law pleads His truth in the threats, sanctions, and curse of the law. It pleads His righteousness, holiness, and severity, all engaged to destroy sinners. But there is a full and satisfactory answer given to this whole plea of the law in salvation, for God declares how He has satisfied all these things, and the exaltation of His glory in them, in and through this way of salvation—as we shall shortly see.

True faith will cling to this in every distress. "Whatever my state and condition may be," says the soul, "whatever my fears and perplexities may be, whatever oppositions I may yet meet, yet in the mirror of the gospel, I see in Jesus Christ, that there is no inconsistency between God's glory and my salvation. This otherwise insurmountable difficulty, with which the law challenged my life and comfort, is erased." So faith approves of this way as that which gives such harmony to both its governing desires, so that it shall not need to forgo either of them and either be contented to be damned that God may be glorified, as some have spoken, or desire salvation without a due regard unto the glory of God. While faith keeps this fortress in the soul, with a constant approval of this way of salvation by Christ, it will be an anchor to stay hold the soul firm in all its storms and distresses.

Some Benefits of Saving Faith

Saving faith benefits the soul in four ways:

1. The soul will be preserved from ruining despair no matter what distresses may befall it. Despair is nothing but a prevalent apprehension that God's glory and a man's salvation are inconsistent—that God cannot be just, true, holy, or righteous if this apprehensive man may be saved. Such a person concludes that his salvation is impossible because, one way or another, it is inconsistent with the glory of God. For nothing else can render it impossible. These thoughts cultivate an utter dislike of God, along with revengeful thoughts against Him for being what He is. This cuts off all endeavors of reconciliation. Yes, this brings about an abhorrence of all the means of reconciliation as being weak, foolish, and insufficient. Such are Christ and His cross to men in this state of mind, fostering these apprehensions. They think Christ and His cross unable to reconcile God's glory and their salvation. When this is so, the soul is in an open entrance into hell. But faith preserves the soul from this frame of mind and ultimate ruin, when it persuades the mind and heart of the consistency and harmony between God's glory and the soul's own salvation. While this persuasion is prevalent in the soul, although it cannot attain any comfortable assurance of a special interest in it, yet it cannot but love, honor, value, and cleave to this way, adoring the wisdom and grace of God in it. And this is an act and evidence of saving faith (see Ps. 130:3–4).

2. Indeed, saving faith will preserve the soul from heartless despondencies. Many—in their temptations, darknesses, and fears, although they do not fall into ruining desperation—fall under such deep fears and various discouragements that they are kept from vigorously seeking to be recovered. Because of this lack of the due exercise of grace, they grow weaker and darker every day and are in danger of pining away in their sins. But faith keeps the soul constant in approving of God's way of saving sinners as that in which God's glory and its own salvation are not only fully reconciled but made inseparable. This will stir up all graces to due exercise and the diligent performance of all duties. By this the soul may obtain a refreshing sense of a personal interest in salvation.

3. Saving faith will also keep the heart full of kindness toward God, from which will spring love and gracious hope. This is impossible for a soul overwhelmed with a sense of sin and thus filled with self-condemnation. But if the soul has a view of the consistency of God's glory with salvation, it must have such kindness toward God and such gracious thoughts of Him that they will kindle love and hope within his soul (Mic. 7:18–20; Ps. 85:8; 1 Tim. 1:15).

4. A steadfast persistence in approving of God's way of salvation, for the reasons already mentioned, will lead the mind into that exercise of faith that both declares

its nature and is the source of all the saving benefits we receive by it. Now, this is such a spiritual light into the declaration made in the gospel of God's wisdom, love, grace, and mercy in Christ, and the way of salvation through Him, that the soul finds them sufficient for its own pardon, righteousness, and salvation. The soul, therefore, places its whole trust and confidence in the gospel for these ends of pardon, righteousness, and salvation.

Three Things Required in Saving Faith

Three things are required of saving faith:

1. A spiritual light into and discovery of the revelation of God's wisdom, love, grace, and mercy in Christ Jesus declared in the gospel. Saving faith requires more than a mere assent to the truth of the revelation or the authority of the revealer; this is already assumed and included in it. But faith adds to this a spiritual discerning, perception, and understanding of what has been revealed and declared. Without this perception, a bare assent to the truth of the revelation is of no advantage. This spiritual perception is called "the light of the knowledge of the glory of God in the face of Jesus Christ" (2 Cor. 4:6). The apostle earnestly prays for the increase of this light in all believers (Eph. 1:15–20). So we discern spiritual things in a spiritual manner, and from this arises "the full assurance of understanding, to the acknowledgment of the mystery of God, and of the Father, and of Christ"

(Col. 2:2); that is, a spiritual sense of the power, glory, and beauty of the things contained in this mystery. This is to know Christ as we know "the power of his resurrection, and the fellowship of his sufferings" (Phil. 3:10).

Faith affects the mind with an inexpressible sense, taste, experience, and acknowledgment of the greatness, the glory, the power, the beauty of the things revealed in salvation. The soul is enabled to see and understand that all aspects of salvation are in accord with God's wisdom, goodness, and love, as we have already declared. A spiritual light that enables this understanding is essential to saving faith. Unless this is in us, we do not truly glorify God, although we may give verbal assent to the truth. Faith is that grace which God has prepared, fitted, and suited to give Him the glory that is His due in the work of our redemption and salvation.

2. Second, the mind of faith, upon receiving this spiritual light regarding the revelation of God and His glory in this way of saving sinners, finds and sees that all things in it are suited to its justification and salvation in particular. But not only is the method fitting—the power of God is in them to make them effectual. The whole blessed event of justification depends on this act and work of faith. It is not enough for a man to see all sorts of food and provisions if they are not in any way suited to his appetite nor fitting for his nourishment. Nor will it be to a man's spiritual advantage to view the excellences of the gospel unless he finds them suited to

his condition. This is the hardest task and work that faith has to do.

Faith is not a special assurance of a man's justification and salvation by Christ. Faith will produce this, but not until it makes further progress. Rather, faith is a persuasion that God's way of salvation proposed in the gospel is suitable and sufficient to save the particular soul that believes. Faith is persuaded not only that this is a blessed way to save sinners in general but also that it is such a way to save him in particular. So the apostle states, "This is a faithful saying, and worthy of all acceptation," or approval, "that Christ Jesus came into the world to save sinners; of whom I am chief" (1 Tim. 1:15). His faith does not stay here or confine itself to this, that Christ Jesus came into the world to save sinners, that this is the holy and blessed way of God for the salvation of sinners in general; but he applies it to himself, saying, "It is God's way, suitable and sufficient, to save me, who am the chief of sinners."

This, as I mentioned, is the greatest and the most difficult work of faith, for we can assume several things about the person who is to believe. First, he is really and effectually convinced of the sin of fallen human nature, of our apostasy from God, the loss of His image, and the dire effects that are the consequences of sin. Second, he has appropriate apprehensions of the holiness and severity of God and the sanction and curse of the law as well as a corresponding understanding of the nature of sin and its demerit. Third, he has a full conviction of his own actual sins, with all their aggravations—from their greatness, their number, and all sorts of circumstances. Fourth, this man has a sense of the guilt of secret or unknown sins, which the continual proneness to sin that he finds working within him has only multiplied. Lastly, he seriously considers what it is to appear before the judgment seat of God and receive a sentence for eternity.

When these things are true with any man, he shall find it the hardest thing in the world, clogged with the most difficulties, for him to believe that the way of salvation proposed unto him is suitable and every way sufficient to save him in particular. He will find it difficult to grasp this truth so fully that no objections can rise up against or stand before him. But this is what the faith of God's elect will do, enabling the soul to discern and satisfy itself that in God's plan there is everything that is necessary for its own salvation. And it will do so on a spiritual understanding and full consideration of three things. First, the infiniteness of God's wisdom, love, grace, and mercy, which is the original or sovereign cause of salvation, with the gospel's plentiful declaration and confirmation of these attributes. Second, the unspeakably glorious way and means for procuring and communicating to us all the effects of this wisdom, grace, and mercy—namely, the incarnation and mediation of the Son of God, in His sacrifice and intercession. And, third, the great multitude and variety of precious promises that engage God's truth, faithfulness, and power in order to communicate the wisdom, love, grace, and mercy of His salvation, made possible by Christ. Upon rightly considering these things, with all the other encouragements that accompany them, the soul concludes by faith that there is salvation for itself in particular, to be attained in this way.

3. The last act of faith, in the order of nature, is the soul's renunciation of all other ways and means for salvation. Jesus Christ is the proper and immediate object of saving faith because He is the life and center of this way in His person, mediation, and righteousness. It is in Christ alone that God will glorify His wisdom, love, grace, and mercy, as it is Christ who has purchased, procured, and wrought all this salvation for us. It is Christ's righteousness that is attributed to us for our justification, and it is Christ who, in carrying out His office, actually bestows His righteousness upon us. This, then, is what Scripture calls believing in Christ: trusting in Him alone for life and salvation, as He administers the whole of divine wisdom and grace for these ends. For this we *come* to Him, *receive* Him, *believe* in Him, *trust* Him, and *abide* in Him. So this way of salvation is essential to the comfort of believers in the midst of all their trials and temptations.

Saving Faith Approves of God's Way of Salvation as That Which Most Honors God's Law

In the third place, faith approves of God's way of saving sinners as that which makes God's glory in the giving and the sanction of the law to be as evident as if every one of us had personally fulfilled it. The law was a just representation of the righteousness and holiness of God, and it was given to be the means of eternally exalting God's glory in these holy properties of His nature. Let no one imagine that God has laid aside this law as useless or that His glory, or any part of it, will be diminished. He designed the law to show His holiness and glory, and heaven and earth shall pass away, but not a jot or tittle of the law. No believer can desire or be pleased with his own salvation unless the glory of God, designed by the law, is secured. A believer cannot desire for God to give up any part of His glory that he might be saved. The believer rejoices in his own salvation chiefly because by it God will be absolutely, universally, and eternally glorified.

Faith sees and understands how the glory God designed for Himself in the giving of the law is eternally and entirely preserved, without eclipse or decrease, by the salvation of sinners through Jesus Christ by mercy, pardon, and the righteousness of another (of all these the law knows nothing). The gospel declares how this may be so (Rom. 3:24–26; 8:2–4; 10:3–4), and faith is enabled to answer all the challenges and charges of the law, with all its pleas for the vindication of divine justice, truth, and holiness. Faith offers that which gives the law the utmost satisfaction in all its pleas for God. We see this answer offered in Romans 8:32–34:

> He that spared not his own Son, but delivered him up for us all, how shall he not with him also freely give us all things? Who shall lay any thing to the charge of God's elect? It is God that justifieth. Who is he that condemneth? It is Christ that died, yea rather, that is risen again, who is even at the right hand of God, who also maketh intercession for us.

So we have seen the first way by which the faith of God's elect shows itself in the minds and consciences of those who believe, in the midst of all their contests with sin, their trials and temptations, and to their relief and comfort. Faith shows itself in embracing and approving God's way of saving sinners by Jesus Christ on the grounds and reasons that have been declared.

CHAPTER 2

Second Evidence: Habitually Approving of the Holiness and Obedience God Requires, as Revealed in Scripture

The second way in which true faith shows itself in the souls and consciences of believers, for their support and comfort in all conflicts with sin in trials and temptations, is by constantly approving of God's revealed will in Scripture concerning our holiness and obedience. This, faith will never forego no matter what trials it may undergo or what darkness the mind may fall into. Faith will abide by this approval of holiness in all situations and circumstances.

We must consider several things in order for this to be seen as a distinctive effect or work of saving faith:

1. There is in all men, by nature, a light that enables them to differentiate moral good and evil, especially in matters of great importance. We do not acquire this light ourselves. We are not taught it. It is not something that we learn. We are born with this light, and

it is inseparable from us. It precedes consideration and reflection, working naturally and necessarily in the first motions of our souls.

This light's power to discern the moral nature of men's actions is inseparably accompanied by a judgment that they make regarding their own actions, whether good or evil. They make this judgment concerning themselves with respect to the superior judgment of God about the same things. The apostle expressly ascribes this to the Gentiles, who did not have the law, in Romans 2:14–15: "The Gentiles, which have not the law, do by nature the things contained in the law, these, having not the law, are a law unto themselves: which shew the work of the law written in their hearts, their conscience also bearing witness, and their thoughts the mean while accusing or else excusing one another." This is a most exact description of a natural conscience's ability to perceive both good and evil, in both of its powers. The conscience both perceives the good and evil that is commanded and the evil that is forbidden in the law, and it passes judgment, either acquitting or condemning, according to what men have done.

This approval of moral duty is thus common to all people. The light by which it is guided may be improved (as it was in some of the Gentiles); or it may be stifled in some, until it seems to be quite extinguished—until they become like the beasts that perish. Furthermore, where the discerning power of this light remains, its judging power may be effectively lost through a persistent and obstinate practice of sin. So the apostle declares concerning those who are judicially hardened and given over to sin in Romans 1:32: "Knowing the judgment of God, that they which commit such things are worthy of death, not only do the same, but have pleasure in them that do them." Though they still discern what is evil and sinful and know the judgment of God concerning such things, they are so overcome with the love of sin and the habit of sinning that they treat with contempt both their own light and God's judgment, so as to delight in what is contrary unto them. These the apostle describes in Ephesians 4:19: "Being past feeling" (all sense of conviction), "[they] have given themselves over unto lasciviousness, to work all uncleanness with greediness," such as the world is filled with today.

This is not that approval of holiness and obedience we're speaking about. This is, in some measure, in the worst of men and has no resemblance to that duty of faith that we are considering, as will shortly become clear.

2. In addition to a discernment of good and evil by the conscience, a second distinctive effect of saving faith is a knowledge of good and evil by the law, accompanied with a judgment, either acquitting or condemning. For the law has the same judging power and authority over men that their own consciences have: the authority of God Himself. To sinners, the law is like the Tree of Knowledge of Good and Evil: it opens their eyes to see

the nature of what they have done, "For by the law is the knowledge of sin" (Rom. 3:20). So also is the knowledge of duty, for the law is the adequate rule of all duty. So the law communicates a knowledge and conviction of duty and sin to men, and this knowledge and conviction is far more clear and distinct than what is in men by the mere light of nature. For the law extends to more occasions regarding duties and sins, occasions that may not occur to us by nature alone. The law also declares the nature of every sin and duty far more clearly than natural light can do by itself.

This knowledge of good and evil by the law may be increased in the minds of men as to press them to perform all known duties and abstain from all known sins, with a judgment on them all. Yet the approval of holiness and obedience that faith produces does not consist in this either, for several reasons.

First, as to the approval or condemnation of good or evil: that which is by the law is particular, with regard to particular duties and sins, as considered according to specific occasions, but does not extend to the whole law absolutely and all that is required in it. I am not saying it is always partial. There is a legal sincerity that may have respect to all known duties and sins, though it is very rare. Hardly shall we find a person merely under the power of the law who does not show an indulgence of some sin and a neglect of some duties. But such a thing is possible. We see this in Paul in his Pharisaism.

He was "touching the righteousness which is in the law, blameless" (Phil. 3:6). He did not allow any known sin or neglect any known duty. Nor could others charge him with any defect in his performance. He was blameless. But even where this is the case, this approval or condemnation is still particular. In other words, men may respect particular duties and avoid particular sins as they occur, but they do not respect the whole righteousness and holiness of the law, as we shall see. A man may, therefore, approve of and execute every duty in its season or, when he thinks of it, by an act of his fixed judgment (and so, on the contrary, as to sin), and yet fall short of the holiness and righteousness after which we inquire.

Second, approval and condemnation is not accompanied with a love of the things themselves that are good and a hatred of those that are sinful. For such persons do not and cannot "delight in the law of God after the inward man" (Rom. 7:22), so as to approve of the law and all that is contained in it and cleave to it with love and delight. Such persons may have a love for this or that duty and a hatred of contrary sins, but it is for various reasons that are simply suited to their convictions and circumstances. It is not because of their formal nature, either good or evil.

Third, no man, therefore, without the light of saving faith, can constantly and universally approve of the revelation of God's will regarding our holiness and obedience.

To make this clear, we must next consider several things: first, the object of this approval (What it is that saving faith approves?); second, the nature of this approval (In what does it consist?); third, the grounds of this approval (concerning God and ourselves); and fourth, the acts, ways, and means by which faith shows this approval.

The Object of This Approval

The holiness and obedience which God requires are not in particular duties, taken alone and by themselves, but the entire agreement of our natures and actions with the will of God. Scripture gives us various descriptions of this because of the variety of gracious operations that coexist in it. Having handled the nature of it at large elsewhere,[1] we should mention some main considerations.

1. The first thing to be considered is its *foundation,* or cause. And the cause is the universal renovation of our natures into the image of God (Eph. 4:24). To put it another way, it is the transformation of our whole souls, in all their faculties and powers, into His likeness, by which we become new creatures—the workmanship of God created in Christ Jesus unto good works (2 Cor. 5:17; Eph. 2:10), in which we are originally and formally sanctified throughout our natures in our "whole spirit

1. Owen, *Pneumatologia,* in *Works,* 3:366–565.

and soul and body" (1 Thess. 5:23). This is the whole law of God written in our hearts, transforming them into the image of the divine holiness that is represented in the law. And this, next to the blood of Christ and His righteousness, is the principal source of peace, rest, and delight to the souls of believers. It is their joy and satisfaction to find themselves restored to a likeness and conformity to God, as we shall further see. Where there is not some gracious sense and experience of this, there is nothing but disorder and confusion in the soul. Nothing can give the soul a sweet composure, a satisfaction in itself, a delight with what it is, except a spiritual sense of this renovation of the image of God in the soul.

2. Next, this holiness may be considered in regard to its *permanent principle* in the mind and affections. Because of its close relationship to Christ, its union with Him, and derivation from Him, this principle is sometimes said to be Christ Himself. Hence we live, yet it is not us, but Christ who lives in us (Gal. 2:20). Jesus said, "Without me ye can do nothing" (John 15:5); He is our life (Col. 3:4). This is a permanent principle of spiritual life, light, love, and power, which acts in the whole soul and all the faculties of the mind, enabling them to cleave to God with purpose of heart and to live for Him in all their spiritual duties. This is how the Holy Ghost is "in [the believer] a well of water springing up into everlasting life" (John 4:14). This principle is the spirit that is born of the Spirit. It is the divine nature, by which we

are made partakers by God's promises. It is a principle of victorious faith and love and brings with it the grace necessary to perform holy obedience, either the matter or manner of their performance. It enables the soul for all the acts of the life of God with joy and delight.

This is its nature. However, as to the degree of its operation and manifestation, it may be very low and weak in some true believers, at least for a season. But all true believers possess, to some degree, a spiritually vital principle of obedience that partakes of the nature of that holiness which we have described. If the believer attends to this principle, it will show itself in its power, to the gracious refreshment and satisfaction of the soul. There are few who so lack these evidences that they cannot say, "Once I was blind, but now I see, though I know not how my eyes were opened. Once I was dead, but now I find motions of a new life in me, in breathing after grace and hungering and thirsting after righteousness, though I know not how I was quickened."

3. This holiness may be considered with regard to its *disposition,* inclinations, and motions, as the first workings of sin are called "the motions of sins" active in us (Rom. 7:5). Therefore, these are the first actions of the vital principle of spiritual life. Such motions and inclinations to obedience work in the minds of believers from this principle of holiness. It produces a constant, invariable disposition to all duties of a godly life. It is a new nature, and a nature cannot lack appropriate inclinations and

motions. This new spiritual disposition consists in a constant delight in that which is good and in accordance with God's will, an adherence by love unto His will, and a readiness and stability of mind with respect to particular duties. David describes it throughout Psalm 119, and Isaiah prophesies concerning the efficacy of the grace of the gospel in changing the natures of those who partake of it (Isa. 11:6–8).

Every believer may ordinarily find this nature in himself. For although indwelling sin and temptation may weaken, oppose, and interrupt it; and though it may be impaired by a neglect of stirring up and exercising the principle of spiritual life in all requisite graces and on all occasions; yet it will still be working in them, and will fill the mind with a constant dissatisfaction with itself, when it is not observed, followed, and improved. No believer will ever have peace of mind if he does not have some experience of a universal disposition toward holiness and godliness in his mind and soul. The psalmist says, "Great peace have they which love thy law: and nothing shall offend them" (Ps. 119:165). It is in this that believers' souls find much delight.

4. This holiness may also be considered with regard to the *acts*, duties, and works, both internal and external, which make up our full obedience. Being made free from sin (by the way previously discussed) and now the servants of God, believers herein have their "fruit unto holiness," of which "the end [is] everlasting life"

(Rom. 6:22). I do not need to stop to describe this. Its characteristics are sincerity in every task and comprehensiveness with respect to all duties. Paul says in 1 Thessalonians 4:3, "This is the will of God, even your sanctification." Pursue "holiness, without which no man shall see the Lord" (Heb. 12:14). We are to approve of "that good, and acceptable, and perfect, will of God" (Rom. 12:2).

The Nature of This Approval

This leads us to ask, What is that approval of this way of holiness that qualifies as an evidence of saving faith? I say that it is an approval that arises from experience and is accompanied by choice, delight, and acceptance. It is when the soul acts in delightful adherence to the whole will of God. It is a settled approval of the beauty and excellence of the holiness and obedience that the gospel reveals and requires.

This approval cannot exist in any unregenerate person who is not under the conduct of saving faith, who is destitute of its light. The apostle assures his reader of this in Romans 8:7: "The carnal mind is enmity against God: for it is not subject to the law of God, neither indeed can be." As long as the mind is carnal or not renewed, it possesses a radical enmity toward God's law. This hostile frame of heart stands in direct opposition to approval of holiness. Their mind may think well of this or that duty because of its conscience and other considerations, and so attend to their performance. But the unregenerate mind utterly dislikes the law itself because it requires universal holiness. All who possess this enmity are "alienated from the life of God through the ignorance that is in them" (Eph. 4:18). The "life of God" consists of the holiness and obedience which He requires of us in principle and duty. To be alienated from it is to dislike and disapprove of it. All unregenerate persons possess this frame of mind.

Having prepared the way, I return to, and confirm, the assertion that *true, saving faith, in all storms and temptations, in all darkness and distress, will show itself, to the comfort and support of them in whom it is, by a constant, universal approval of the whole will of God concerning our holiness and obedience, both in general and in every particular instance of it.* We can further explain this in two parts.

1. Faith will not allow the mind, on any occasion or temptation, to entertain the least dislike of holiness, or of anything that belongs to it. The mind may sometimes, through temptations, fall into doubt and apprehension of eternal ruin due to a lack of compliance with the law. This makes the mind displeased with itself, but not with the obedience that God requires. Romans 7:10, 12 says, "The commandment, which was ordained to life, I found to be unto death...[but] the law is holy, and the commandment holy, and just, and good." The regenerate mind reasons, "However it is with me, whatever becomes

of me, though I die and perish, yet the law is holy, just, and good." The mind does not dislike anything in God's will, though it cannot perfectly follow it. Sometimes the conscience is distressed and under rebuke for sin. Sometimes the rebellion of the flesh against duties that defy its natural inclinations burden the mind. Sometimes the world threatens danger in the face of the performance of some religious duties. But none of these are able to provoke the soul that is under the conduct of faith to dislike or to think worse of any of the ways and duties that provoke these difficulties.

2. Furthermore, as the soul will not dislike any part of holiness, so it will not ever desire that it be altered or that its requirements be lessened. Naaman the Syrian liked the worship of the true God in general, but he desired a lessening of duty, in compliance with his earthly interest. This revealed his hypocrisy. Men may imagine that if they could be excused in this or that instance regarding duties that they find dangerous and troublesome (like profession in the times of persecution), or if they could indulge in whatever sin their inclinations are very prone unto or that the world calls them to, they should be happy enough to obey other parts of the law. Many men act in this very way. They *profess* religion and obedience to God but withhold their hearts from full obedience. They will hide a wedge in their tents, indulging some corruption or dislike of some duties. They set their own measure of obedience, and they desire that

God make the standard according to men's practice, not His holy nature. They desire that whatever practice pleases them should also please God. Faith abhors this. The soul that is under the conduct of saving faith is not capable of any desire that does not conform to the will of God concerning its holiness and obedience. It can no more desire this than it can desire that God should not be God. No, though man should imagine that by some change and lessening of God's law in some instances the soul might be saved, saving faith will not allow such an arrangement. Rather, it will choose to stand or fall in regard to the entire will of God.

The Grounds of This Approval

On what ground does faith approve of the whole will of God concerning our holiness and obedience? There are two grounds: one concerning God and one concerning our own souls.

The First Ground of This Approval: Concerning God

Faith looks on the holiness required of us as that which is suited to God's own holiness. It recognizes that it is fitting for God to require this holiness because of His own nature and its infinite perfections. The rule is, "Be ye holy; for I am holy" (1 Peter 1:16). In other words, God requires of us that which reflects His own holiness. Because He is holy, it is necessary that we should be holy. If we belong to Him in a special manner, then our holiness must fit that which His holiness requires.

We have already declared what this gospel holiness is, of what it consists, and what it requires; these may all be considered either as they are in us (that is, inherent in us and performed by us) or as they are in themselves (that is, in their own nature and in God's will). In us, I acknowledge that they do not give a completely clear representation of God's holiness because of our weaknesses, our imperfections, our partial renovation in the degree of our holiness in this life, and our many defects and sins. The picture regenerate Christians paint of holiness, however, is the best image (even in the weakest of believers) that this world can offer. In themselves, in their own nature, according to the will of God, they make up the most glorious representation of God that He has, or ever will, grant in this world. This is especially true if we consider Christ's incarnate exemplification of holiness in the human nature. The holiness that is in believers is of the same nature that was and is in Jesus Christ, although His holiness inconceivably exceeds theirs in the degree of its perfection.

Therefore, God requires us to be holy as He is holy, and perfect as our heavenly Father is perfect. We could not be holy or perfect unless our holiness and perfection bore some resemblance to God's holiness and perfection, and if we bore a correct sense of this continually in our hearts, it would influence us to show greater care and diligence in all instances of duty and sin than we generally show. If we never failed to sincerely and severely call ourselves to analyze whether our frames and actions properly resembled God's holiness and perfections, it would prove a spiritual preservative.

Faith, then, discerns God's likeness in every part of this holiness. Faith sees that it is fitting for God to require holiness, and, on this basis, faith approves of it and reverences God in it. It does this in all the parts of it and in everything that belongs to it, including the form, the acts, and the duties of holiness.

1. Faith principally discerns God's likeness in the inward *form* of holiness (which we have already described); that is, in the new creature, the new nature, or the restitution of the image of God that is in the new nature. In the beauty of this inward form of holiness, faith continually beholds God's likeness and glory, for it is created *kata theon*—according to God, after Him, in His image, "in righteousness and true holiness" (Eph. 4:24). "The new man...is renewed in knowledge after the image of him that created him" (Col. 3:10).

When God created all things, the heavens and the earth with all that is contained in them, He left on them impressions of His infinite wisdom, goodness, and power so that they might declare His perfection—His eternal power and Godhead. Yet He did not create them in His own image. They were only a passive illustration of Him in the light of others, not in themselves. Nor did they at all represent that in which God will be principally glorified among His creatures—namely, the universal rectitude of His nature in righteousness and holiness. Only man was uniquely formed in the image and likeness of God. This was because, in the holiness of his nature, he represented the righteousness of God. But sin lost this, and man in his fallen condition no longer represents God's holiness. There is nothing in him that has anything of the likeness or image of God in it. All is dead, dark, perverse, and confused.[2] God creates this new nature, of which we speak, for this very purpose, that it may be a blessed image and representation of His holiness and righteousness. That is why it is called the "divine nature," of which we are partakers (2 Peter 1:4).

---

2. In his treatise on the Holy Spirit, Owen defines the image of God as "habitual conformity unto God, his mind and will, wherein the holiness and righteousness of God himself was represented." *Pneumatologia,* in *Works,* 3:285. This accounts for why he speaks of God's image being lost. Reformed theology, however, has usually followed Scripture in recognizing that even fallen human beings continue to bear the image of God in some respects. According to Herman Bavinck, "Reformed theologians...speak of the image of God in a broader and narrower sense. In Holy Scripture they read that man, on one hand, is still called the image of God after the fall and should be respected as such (Gen. 5:1; 9:6; Acts 17:28; 1 Cor. 11:3; James 3:9); and that, on the other hand, he had nevertheless lost the primary content of the image of God (i.e., knowledge, righteousness, and holiness) and only regains these qualities in Christ (Eph. 3:24; Col. 3:10)." Herman Bavinck, *Reformed Dogmatics, Vol. 2: God and Creation,* ed. John Bolt, trans. John Vriend (Grand Rapids: Baker Academic, 2006), 550. Owen is using "image of God" in this second, narrower sense.

He who cannot see a representation of God in this new nature does not possess the light of faith.

It is on this basis that faith approves of the form and principle of this holiness, as the renovation of the image of God in us. It recognizes that God bestowing on and requiring this holiness of us is fitting for Him, and so it is incomparably excellent and desirable. Indeed, when the soul is ready to faint under doubt that it is a partaker of this holy nature because of the power of sin in the soul and temptations on it; when it knows not whether itself be born of God or not (as is the case with many); yet wherever this faith is present it will discern the beauty and glory of the new creation, in some measure, as that which bears the image of God. And because of this, faith preserves a longing after holiness, or a farther participation of it, in the soul.

Faith, by this work or act, discovers its sincerity, which is what this book inquires after. When faith's eyes are open to behold the glory of God in the new creature, when it sees it as that which mirrors God's own holiness and recognizes it as a becoming requirement, it can then approve of it as excellent and desirable, and it will be an anchor to the soul in its greatest storms. For saving faith is a work beyond what a mere enlightened conscience can produce.[3] An enlightened conscience can approve or

3. Owen is using the word "enlightened" in a different sense than he was earlier. Here Owen has in mind the person who has experienced some measure of conviction but has not fully embraced

disapprove of all the acts and effects of obedience and disobedience when it regards their consequences, but faith alone discerns the spiritual nature of the new creature, as it represents God's holiness, and, on this basis, faith constantly approves of it.

2. Faith does the same thing concerning the internal *acts* and effects of this new creature, this principle of new obedience. The first thing it produces in us is a spiritual and heavenly frame of mind. Those who walk according to the Spirit are "spiritually minded" (Rom. 8:5–6). It looks on the opposite state—being carnally minded—as vile and hateful, for the carnal mind is ready and disposed to act on the lusts of the flesh. But in a constellation of all the graces of the Spirit influencing, disposing, and equipping the soul to carry out these graces, this spiritual frame of mind is the inward glory of the "king's daughter" (Ps. 45:13). Faith views whatever is contrary to the spiritual frame as vile, base, and unworthy of God or of those who aim to enjoy Him.

3. Faith does the same concerning all internal and external particular *duties,* when the Spirit enlivens and fills them with grace. Our walking worthy of God (Col. 1:10; 1 Thess. 2:12) consists in these duties—a walk that is fitting for God to accept and in which we glorify

---

Christ in saving faith. This is evident in how Owen sets the "merely enlightened conscience" in contrast to "saving faith."

Him. On the other hand, faith condemns and abhors the neglect of duties of holiness or the performance of duties without the proper exercise of grace; it is unworthy of God, unworthy of our high and holy calling, and unworthy of our profession.

As we observed before, faith will continue to do all this constantly, even under temptations and desertions. There are seasons in which the soul may be very weak in the powers, effects, and duties of this spiritual life. The psalmist often complains of this in his own case, and it is evident in most people's experience. There are only few who have not found, at one time or another, great weakness, decay, and deadness in their spiritual condition. Sometimes true believers may lack any refreshing experience of faith's operations. They may not be able to determine whether sin or grace has the dominion in them. Yet even in all these seasons faith will keep the soul in constant approval of this holiness and obedience, in its root and fruits, principle and effects, nature, disposition, and duties. For when believers cannot see the beauty of these things in themselves, they can see it in the promises of the covenant, in the truth of the gospel in which it is declared, and in its effects in others.

By this, faith obtains several great advantages. This exercise of saving faith will never allow the heart to be at rest in any sinful way or under any such spiritual decay as estrange it from the pursuit of holiness. The sight of holiness, the conviction of its excellence, and the approval of it, which answers the holiness of God, will cause the mind to endeavor after it and will rebuke the soul for neglect of it. Nor will faith allow any quiet or peace within unless it endeavors after a comforting assurance of holiness. The soul that has lost an abiding sense of the excellence of this holiness, which befits the holiness and will of God, is desperately sick. Fears and checks of conscience are the only security against the worst of sins, and they are not a sufficient replacement for the peace of God.

This is one great difference between believers and those who have no faith. The minds of unbelievers, in all they do toward God or for eternity, are guided by fear of the consequences of sin, with an understanding of some advantages that are to be obtained by a respectable life and the profession of religion. But the minds of believers are influenced by a view of the glory of the image and likeness of God in their holiness, to which they are called. This gives them love for holiness, along with delight in it, and enables them to look upon holiness as its own reward. And without these affections no one will ever persevere in the ways of obedience to the end.

Where faith is in this exercise it will also bring relief to the soul in all its darkness and temptations. As long as it continues to approve of the holiness God requires, the mind can never conclude that it is wholly without God and His grace. This is not of ourselves. By nature we are ignorant of it. This "life is hid with Christ in God"

(Col. 3:3), where we cannot see it. In our own nature, we are "alienated from the life of God through the ignorance that is in [us]" (Eph. 4:18). Most men live all their days in contempt of the chief duties of man toward God and of the principle of them, which they look on as a fable. Therefore, the mind may have great satisfaction in a sight of the beauty and approval of this holiness, as that which only sincere and saving faith can produce.

The Second Ground of This Approval: Concerning Ourselves

Second, faith approves of this way of holiness and obedience as that which gives rectitude and perfection to our nature of which it is capable in this world. This way of holiness is the only rule and measure of sanctification, and whatever is contrary to this way is perverse, crooked, vile, and base. Some men think that their nature is capable of no other perfection but what consists in the satisfaction of their lusts. They do not know any other satisfaction, nothing that suits their desires except the pursuit of corrupt lusts and pleasures. So the apostle describes them in Ephesians 4:19: "Being past feeling [they] have given themselves over unto lasciviousness, to work all uncleanness with greediness." The occupation of their lives is to accommodate the flesh, to fulfill its sinful desires. They walk in the lusts of the flesh, "fulfilling" (so far as they are able) "the desires of the flesh and of the mind" (Eph. 2:3). They neither know nor understand what a hell of confusion, disorder, and base degeneracy from their original constitution fills their minds. This perverse satisfaction is nothing but the next inclination to hell, and it manifests its own vileness to everyone who has the least ray of spiritual light.

Some among the heathen placed the improvement of human nature in moral virtues and operations, according to them. This is the highest level to which natural light could ever rise up, but the light of the gospel uncovers its uncertainty and ineffectiveness.

Faith alone discovers what is good for us, in us, and to us while we are in this world. The goodness, the perfection, the order, the present blessedness of our nature consists only in God's renovation of His image in us; in acting according to a gracious principle of spiritual life; in duties and operations suited to such a life; and in the participation of the divine nature by God's promises.

This is how the faculties of our souls are exalted, elevated, and enabled to display their original, unfallen powers with respect to God and our enjoyment of Him, which is our chief end and greatest source of blessing. Only God by His goodness—God as revealed in Jesus Christ by the gospel—redirects our affections on their proper objects. The satisfaction, order, and rest of our affections relies on us embracing holiness. This is how God brings all the powers of our souls into a blessed state and harmony in all their operations, while whatever is dark, perverse, unquiet, vile, and base He casts out. But we must distinctly explain these things a little more.

1. The spring and principle of gospel holiness is a spiritual, saving light, which enables the mind to know God in Christ and to discern spiritual things in a spiritual, saving manner. For herein God shines "in our hearts, to give the light of the knowledge of the glory of God in the face of Jesus Christ" (2 Cor. 4:6). Without this in some degree, there is no true holiness, nothing God accepts, whatever pretense or appearance of holiness there may be. Blind devotion, destitute of this light that illuminates religious duties, will cause men to multiply duties, especially duties of their own invention, in "a shew of wisdom in will worship, and humility, and neglecting of the body," as the apostle says in Colossians 2:23. But there is no gospel holiness in this.

"The new man...is renewed in knowledge after the image of him that created him" (Col. 3:10), says Paul. In the description he gives of evangelical holiness and obedience (both its beginning and progress), Paul explains that this saving light and knowledge is the spring and principle of all real evangelical holiness and obedience, and in Colossians 1:9–11 he declares, "[We] desire that ye might be filled with the knowledge of his will in all wisdom and spiritual understanding; that ye might walk worthy of the Lord unto all pleasing, being fruitful in every good work, and increasing in the knowledge of God; strengthened with all might, according to his glorious power, unto all patience and longsuffering with joyfulness." This is a blessed account of the gospel holiness in its nature, origin, spring, progress, fruits, and effects. A serious consideration of it, in the light of faith, will show how distant and different this holiness is from those schemes of moral virtues that some would substitute in its place. It has a glory in it that no unenlightened mind can see or understand. Its foundation is laid in the knowledge of the will of God in all wisdom and spiritual understanding. This is the spiritual, saving light of which we speak. In Ephesians 1:17–18 the apostle prays for this light to increase in believers: "that the God of our Lord Jesus Christ, the Father of glory, may give unto you the spirit of wisdom and revelation in the knowledge of him: the eyes of your understanding being enlightened; that ye may know what is the hope of his calling, and...the riches of the glory of his inheritance in the saints." In Colossians Paul calls this "increasing in the knowledge of God" (1:10). Here, Paul declares, most illustriously, the singular glory of this saving light's origin, causes, use, and effects. This light is in every true believer and is the only immediate spring of all gospel holiness and obedience. For "the new man...is renewed in knowledge after the image of him that created him" (Col. 3:10).

This light, this wisdom, this spiritual understanding communicated to believers is the perfection of their minds in this world. It gives them order, peace, and power, enabling them to act all their faculties in a due manner, with respect unto their being and end. This light also gives beauty and glory to the inward man and qualifies a believer as an inhabitant of the kingdom of light, whereby we are "delivered...from the power of darkness, and...translated...into the kingdom of his dear Son" (Col. 1:13), "out of darkness into his marvellous light" (1 Peter 2:9).

Scripture declares that everything contrary to this—ignorance, darkness, blindness, and vanity—is in the minds of all unregenerate persons who have not been cured by God's glorious working of His power and grace, which was previously mentioned.

Now, faith discerns these things, as the spiritual man discerns all things (1 Cor. 2:15). It sees the beauty of this heavenly light and recognizes its power to give order and uprightness to the mind. Faith also discerns that whatever is contrary to this light is vile, base, horrid, and shameful. As for those who "loved darkness rather than light, because their deeds were evil" (John 3:19), it knows they are strangers to Christ and His gospel.

2. Again, God requires a principle of spiritual life and love for Him in this holiness. This guides, acts, and rules in the soul in all its obedience and gives the soul proper direction in every circumstance. Whatever is contrary to this is death and enmity against God. Faith judges between these two principles and their operations: it approves of the former in all its outworking as lovely, beautiful, and desirable—that which is the uprightness

and perfection of the will. The latter principle faith sees as deformed and perverse.

3. We may say the same of its nature and operations in the soul's affections and of all the duties of obedience which proceed from it.

The Acts, Ways, and Means by Which Faith Shows Its Approval

Our only remaining task is to show the acts, ways, and means by which faith evidences its approval of gospel holiness. Faith considers it lovely and desirable in itself, for holiness sanctifies our minds to the furthest extent possible in this world. Faith evidences its approval in two ways.

1. By self-dissatisfaction and humiliation, which it stirs up any time the mind falls short of this holiness. This is the chief principle and cause of holy shame, which befalls believers on every sin—"those things whereof ye are now ashamed" (Rom. 6:21). When you see by the light of faith how vile sin is, how unworthy of you, and what a debasement of your souls there is in sin, you are ashamed of it. It is true: the chief cause of holy shame is a sense of the unsuitableness of sin in the face of God's holiness and the horrible ingratitude and insincerity that sin shows toward Him. But the fact that sin is a thing unworthy of us and that in which our natures are exceedingly debased is also a significant source of this

shame. God says, through Isaiah, that wicked sinners "debase [themselves] even unto hell" (Isa. 57:9); or make themselves as vile as hell itself by ways unworthy of man's nature. This is one reason for severe self-reflections that accompany godly sorrow for sin (2 Cor. 7:11).

The sincerity of faith is especially evident when the believer is ashamed of himself every time he comes short of the holiness God requires. Although no eye sees his sins but his own and God's, a regenerate man has an inward shame and sorrow for sin that grows on no other root than sincere faith. Whatever conflicts, therefore, sin may be waging in and against our souls, whatever decays we may fall into (these are the two principles of darkness and fear in believers), as long as inward holy shame and godly sorrow for sin is preserved, faith is evident in us.

2. Faith also shows its approval of holiness through a spiritual satisfaction, which it gives the soul in every experience of the transforming power of holiness, conforming it more and more to God's own. Secret joy and spiritual refreshment rise in the soul from the sense of its renovation into the image of God, and all sanctification only increases this joy. This is the soul's gradual return to its upright created order, with the blessed addition of supernatural light and grace by Christ Jesus. This is how the soul finds itself coming home to God from its old apostasy, in the way of approaching eternal

rest and blessedness. And there is no satisfaction like the satisfaction it receives in this.

This is the second way in which faith will abide firm and constant and show itself in the soul of every believer. However low and weak the accomplishments of its spiritual life, even though it is overwhelmed with darkness and a sense of the guilt of sin and surprised and perplexed with the deceit and violence of sin, faith will continue firm and unshaken. It sees the glory and excellence of the holiness and obedience that God requires as a representation of God's own glorious excellence, the renovation of His image, and thereby the perfection of our natures. It constantly approves of this holiness, even in the soul's deepest trials, and while this anchor holds firm and stable we are safe.

CHAPTER 3

Third Evidence: Consistently Endeavoring to Keep All Grace in Exercise in All Ordinances of Divine Worship

The third way in which saving faith shows itself is by a diligent, constant endeavor to keep itself and all grace in exercise in all ordinances of divine worship, both private and public. The due exercise of inward grace is the touchstone of faith and spiritual obedience, and it is the most intimate and difficult part of worship. Where this is missing there is no life in the soul. There are two ways men deceive themselves in this.

First, abounding in the performance of duties or a multiplication of duties. This is how hypocrites have in all ages deceived themselves (Isa. 58:2–3). The Church of Rome used outward show to cover its apostasy from the gospel—an endless multiplication of religious duties in which they trusted and boasted. We may often find men who pretend conscientiousness regarding their observation of outward duties, and yet they will embrace every sin that meets their lusts. Men may, and often do, unwaveringly perform their duties, especially in their families and in public. They may multiply duties beyond the ordinary measure, hoping in this way to approve themselves in lusts and neglects.

The second way men deceive themselves is through the assistance of gifts in the performance of duties.[1] But in these things there is not one ounce of saving grace, so when man rests in them, they keep the soul in formality to ruin all workings of grace and to bring an incurable hardness on the whole soul.

---

1. Owen's meaning here is somewhat vague. In one of his sermons, Owen warned that "the profession of religion, and the performance of duties, under a world-like conversation, are nothing but a sophistical means to lead men blindfold into hell." Sermon 7, in *The Works of John Owen*, ed. W. H. Goold (Edinburgh: Banner of Truth, 1966), 8:331. In another sermon, Owen said that a prevalent corruption is not "inconsistent with the performance of duties; but it is inconsistent with the true exercise of grace in the performance of duties. It is often seen and known, that persons under prevalent corruption will multiply duties, thereby to quiet conscience, and to compensate God for what they have done amiss. Persons may multiply prayers, follow preaching, and attend to other duties, when they use all these things, through the deceitfulness of sin, but as a cloak unto some prevailing corruption; but in all those duties there is no true exercise of grace." Sermon 9, in *Works*, 8:387. These statements indicate that Owen has in mind those who rely on the outward performance of spiritual duties while neglecting the inward exercise of grace. By "assistance of gifts," Owen may be thinking of outward helps for worship, such as music or ceremony. As a contemporary illustration, we might think of someone who is caught up in the music of a song during worship, but gives little thought to actually directing faith toward Christ while singing.

Wherever faith is sincere, it will constantly strive to fulfill all duties of divine worship with a living, real heart that acts in grace. Where it does not do this, faith will never allow the soul to gain any rest or satisfaction in such duties but will cast them away as a defiled garment. He who can perform such duties without endeavoring for the real exercise of grace in them, and without disregard of self, will not find any other clear evidence of saving faith in himself.

The Consequences of Neglecting to Keep Grace in Exercise

There are three evils that have ruined multitudes and have followed the ignorance, neglect, or weariness of exercising grace through public and private worship.

1. Neglect of these duties was and is the origin of all false worship and has sparked man's invention of false worship's superstitious rites and ceremonies. Having lost the exercise of faith in the divinely instituted ordinances of worship, men found that it was useless and burdensome. For without the constant exercise of faith there is no life in it or satisfaction to be obtained by it. People must have something in it or accompanying it that will entertain their minds and engage their affections. If worship also lacked these things, as well as the exercise of faith, not one person would practice even false worship. This is why men invented various forms of prayer with continual diversions to distract the mind from why this is the case:

because the mind cannot continue in spiritual pursuits without the exercise of faith. The mere performance of these diversions entertain the mind, causing it to think that there is something where, in fact, there is nothing. Men add outward ceremonies of robes, postures, and gestures of veneration for the same reason. Their only purpose is to entertain the mind and emotions with some delight and satisfaction in outward worship, which the lack of the exercise of faith, the life and soul of worship in believers, has voided of all meaning. When anyone finds decay in their worship, they shall find themselves sinking down into the use of these lifeless forms. Or else they will sink into exercising their natural faculties and memory, which is not one jot better. Some, from an eminency in spiritual gifts and the performing duties by virtue of them, have sunk into an Ave Maria[2] or a Credo.[3]

2. By neglecting proper worship, many have turned aside, fallen away from, and forsaken the solemn ordinances of divine worship, instead turning to vain imaginations for relief, in trembling, excited singing, and false raptures. This is why so many have forsaken their own mercies to follow after lying vanities. For a while, they observed the divine institutions of worship, but having no faith to exercise in them, by which alone the

2. A traditional Roman Catholic prayer invoking the intercession of the virgin Mary.

3. A recitation of the Apostles' Creed.

institutions have life and power, the institutions became useless and burdensome to them. They could not find any sweetness, satisfaction, or benefit in them. It is not possible that so many in our days, if ever they had tasted true worship, should go after new, false practices. If they experienced the savor, power, and life that are found in the ordinances of divine worship when they are performed and enlivened by faith, they would not forsake them for emptiness. "They went out from us, but they were not of us; for if they had been of us, they would no doubt have continued with us" (1 John 2:19). "Had they known it, they would not have crucified the Lord of glory" (1 Cor. 2:8). This, therefore, is the true reason why so many in our days, after they have lived in the observation of the gospel ordinances of worship for a time, have fallen away from them. Having no faith to exercise in them and not seeking after true faith, they found no life or benefit in them.

3. For the same reason, some fall into profaneness, practicing a natural religion without any instituted worship at all. There are many of these people in our day and age. There is no trace of the light of faith in them, so they cannot see any beauty in Christ or in anything that belongs to Him. So, every day, many souls hasten to their ruin.

True faith will show itself in all darkness and distress whatsoever. It will always endeavor to keep itself and all other graces in a right and constant practice of worship, private and public. It may sometimes be weakened in its acting and operations. It may be under decays. It may be as asleep, not only in particular times or duties, but in the entire frame of mind. But where faith is true and genuine, it will shake off the dust, cast off the sin that so easily besets us, and stir itself up to its duty with might and contention. The most dangerous place for a soul is when it is sinking down into formality, neglecting to exercise its faith, in a multitude of duties. Then it is ready to die, if it is not already dead.

If we are wise, therefore, we will keep watch and take care that we do not lose this evidence of faith. It may help us when all other things seem against us. Some, finding themselves at desperation's door, are relieved when they remember this exercise of faith. They remember some season in which they experienced the work of faith in prayer which brought them relief. An experience of this exercise of faith is like a jewel. While it may be useless when locked up in a cabinet, you know its value if you ever come to need bread for your lives.

The Means for Keeping Grace in Exercise

It is, therefore, worthwhile to inquire what we ought to do, by which means, to keep faith in due exercise in all the parts of divine worship so that it may comfort us in times of temptation and darkness. The following directions may be useful:

1. Labor to keep a sense of the divine nature's infinite perfections in your heart and in all your approaches to

God. Think especially of God's sovereign power, holiness, immensity, and omnipresence. This will instill in us a sense of humility because of our infinite distance from Him. The Scripture gives us descriptions of God that foster this frame of mind. Joshua aimed to instill it in the Israelites when he sought to engage them in worship (Josh. 24:19–22). In the New Testament, the writer to the Hebrews implores his readers similarly: "Wherefore we receiving a kingdom which cannot be moved, let us have grace, whereby we may serve God acceptably with reverence and godly fear: for our God is a consuming fire" (12:28–29). Glorious descriptions and appearances of God are numerous in Scripture and fulfill this same purpose. If we fail on all occasions to fill our minds with reverent thoughts of God and His greatness and holiness, then faith has no foundation to stand on when it attempts to exercise the duties of worship. This is the only way into the right exercise of grace. A lack of it shuts all holy thoughts and affections out of our minds. Where it is present, grace will undoubtedly work in our hearts in all our duties. If we do not possess this when we go to worship, either in our closets or with the congregation, other things will fill our minds and hinder us. Reverent thoughts of God, in our approaches to Him, will cast out all rampant wickedness and dispel carnal and ritualistic mindsets, which will spoil all our duties. Keep your hearts, therefore, under this charge when you approach God, and it will open a door to true worship.

This mindset will also impart a sense of our infinite distance from Him and give us another way to stir up faith to proper reverence and godly fear. This is how Abraham felt (Gen. 18:27), and the wise man, the writer of Ecclesiastes, also directs us to it (Eccl. 5:2). Carnal boldness void of these things ruins men's souls, making all their duties of worship unacceptable to God and unprofitable to themselves.

2. To keep faith in right worship, make your heart aware of how unsuitable even your best duties are in light of God's holiness and majesty, and remind your heart of His infinite condescension[4] in accepting them. Imagine the best and the most lively exercise of grace that we can attain to, the most fervency in prayer, with the most diligent focus of our minds, the most humility and contrite trembling in hearing the Word, and the most devout affection of our minds in all parts of worship. Alas! What is all this to God? It cannot answer His infinite holiness (Job 4:18–19; 15:15–16)! Our goodness does not come anywhere close (Ps. 16:2). There is no measure or proportion between the holiness of God and our best duties. There is iniquity in our holy things. Our best duties, just like our persons, have need of mercy and pardon, of cleansing and justification, by the blood of

4. The word "condescension" denotes the act of a superior person descending to the level of an inferior. In Owen's usage, it does not connote a patronizing attitude of smugness.

Christ. God must condescend to take any notice of us or our duties, and we should live in holy admiration of His infinite condescension all our days.

If this is true regarding our best duties and in our best frames, it is an outrage of sloth and negligence for us to bring the carcass of duties to God, neglecting to stir up faith to its due exercise in them. How great is this folly, how unspeakable is the guilt of this negligence! Let us, therefore, keep a sense of this upon our hearts that we may always stir ourselves up to our best in duties of religious worship.

3. Negligence in stirring up faith to a due exercise in all duties of worship is the highest insult we can make to God. Such negligence argues a great disregard of Him. As long as it is true of us, we do not and cannot have a full sense of any of the perfections of the divine nature. Instead of worshiping God, we turn to an idol, assuming that He may be put off with the outside and appearance of things. The apostle cautions us against it (Heb. 4:12–13) and God detests it (Isa. 29:13), calling him a deceiver and cursed who offers the lame and blind to God while he has a male in the flock (Mal. 1:14). Yet this is what we do, to some degree, whenever we neglect to stir up faith in holy duties. Only the stirring up of faith to proper exercise renders our worship "the male of the flock" and makes it an acceptable sacrifice to God. Without faith, our duties are "lame and blind"—a corrupt thing.

For men to neglect their duties, to put themselves to trouble and expense in multiplying duties and attending to them to no purpose, is a sad thing. But it is much sadder, then, when the duties are all insults to God's glory, when they increase the formality and hardness of men's hearts toward the ruin of their souls! "Stand in awe," therefore, "and sin not: commune with your own heart" (Ps. 4:4). Do not cease until, on all occasions, you bring your hearts into that exercise of faith whereby you may glorify God as God, and not as an idol.

4. To this same end, always keep your souls deeply affected with a sense of the things in which you deal with God in all the duties of worship. These fall into two categories: those which concern His glory, and those which concern our own souls. Without a constant due sense of these things in our hearts, faith will not rightly exercise itself in any of our duties. Without this intimate concern and deep sense, we do not know whether or not we are exercising faith in our prayers. Formality will drown all. Our best prayer is but an expression to God of our awareness of these things. If we have no sense at all, then we do not pray at all, whatever we say or do. But when these things dwell in our minds, when we think on them continually, and when our hearts cleave to them, faith will be at work in all our approaches to God. Can you not pray? Charge your hearts with these things, and you will learn to do so.

5. Watch diligently against those things that you know by experience are prone to hinder your fervency in duties. These include carnal reluctance and weariness of the flesh; distracting, foolish daydreams; the occasions of life revolving in our minds; and the like. If we do not remove such obstacles and guard against them, they will influence the mind and its exercise of faith.

6. Finally, above all, the principal rule in this is to always carefully remember Christ in these duties, with respect unto His office. He is the high priest over the house of God: through Him and under His conduct, we are always to draw near to God. It is Christ's work to present the prayers and supplications of the church to God. Our only way to come to Christ for intercession on our behalf is by faith. In all our duties of holy worship we declare that we come to God by Him as our high priest. If we do not endeavor to exercise our faith in this, we mock Him and make a show to Him of doing that which we do not even attempt. There can be no greater contempt of Christ in His office nor a greater undervaluation of His love. When we rightly consider how Christ is concerned in all our duties, it directly leads faith into its proper exercise. For we believe in God through Christ carrying out His office as Mediator. And when the mind is full of proper thoughts of Christ, if there is anything of true saving faith in the heart, it will act rightly to its own benefit and blessing.

These things may be of use to stir us up and guide us to exercise our faith in all holy duties. When experience of this faith abides in the soul, we will see evidence of it, and it will support and comfort in all temptations and distresses.

Some may say that they are not gifted in prayer, that they cannot express themselves with earnestness and fervency, and so they may say they cannot know whether there is any faith in their prayers or not. I answer that this is false, for grace may often be very high where gifts are very low.

Some may complain that those with whom they meet to pray have so small a gift of prayer that they cannot accompany them in the exercise of any grace. But I raise four objections. First, there is no doubt that there is a great difference between men as to their spiritual gift of prayer; some are much more effectual for edification than others. But, second, make sure you are called in providence and duty to join with those you seek to meet with so that you do not first voluntarily choose anything to your disadvantage and then complain of it. Third, no matter how scarce their gift of prayer, if they exercise grace in their own hearts through it, grace will be exercised in ours as well. Where there is no evidence of grace in prayer, I confess the situation is hard. Fourth, and last, fix your mind on the subject matter of the prayer so as to recognize and exercise your faith in what is real in the prayer. In this, it will find its proper work.

CHAPTER 4

Fourth Evidence: Bringing the Soul into a Special State of Repentance

We now come, in the fourth place, to describe a special way by which true faith shows itself not on all, but some occasions: by bringing the soul into a state of repentance. Three things need to be asked and addressed: First, what, in general, do I intend by this state of repentance? Second, what are the times and occasions, or who are the persons, in which faith will do this? And third, what duties are required in it?

What Is This Special State of Repentance?

First, by this state of repentance I do not mean merely the grace and duty of evangelical repentance, for that is absolutely inseparable from true faith and is as necessary for salvation as faith itself. He who does not genuinely repent of sin is not a true believer, no matter what he professes to believe. But here I mean something that is special and not common to all, by which faith, on occasion, shows its power and sincerity.

This state of repentance, however, is of the same *nature* as gospel repentance. There are not two kinds of true repentance, nor are there two different states of those who truly repent. But by this special state of repentance I mean an eminent *degree* of gospel repentance in the habit or root and in its fruits and effects.

There are various degrees in the power and exercise of gospel graces, and some may be more eminent in one and some in another. For example, Abraham and Peter were noteworthy in faith, while David and John were eminent in love. There may also be causes and occasions for the greater and higher exercise of some graces and duties at one time than at another, for we are to attend to duties according to our circumstances in order that we may glorify God in them and benefit our own souls. So the apostle James directs us in James 5:13: "Is any among you afflicted? let him pray. Is any merry? let him sing psalms." Various states and circumstances call for a special, constant, prevalent exercise of several graces and the diligent performance of several duties, especially repentance, in an extraordinary manner.

What Sorts of People Need This Special State of Repentance?

We must consider the categories of people in whom this special degree of repentance is required, by which faith will show itself. There are six sorts of people.

1. Those who have been surprised into great sins by the power of their corruptions and temptations. We have precedents both in the Old Testament and in the New that some true believers may be surprised into great sins, such as uncleanness, drunkenness, gluttony, theft, premeditated lying, oppression in dealing, and failing in profession in the time of persecution. The primitive church believed that the latter type could only recover by faith acting itself in a state of repentance. Such sin has great sorrows, as we see in Peter and the incestuous Corinthian, who was in danger of being "swallowed up with overmuch sorrow" (2 Cor. 2:7). Where any have stumbled in such surprising sin, true faith will immediately work for a recovery by thorough humiliation and repentance, as it did in Peter. In the cases of those who stay longer under the power of sin because of lack of effectual convictions, it will cost them dear in the end, as it did David. But in this case, for the most part, faith will not be content to merely set the broken bone—nor with such a recovery as gives them peace with God and their own consciences. Faith will also incline the soul to a humble, contrite frame; to a mournful walk; and to the universal exercise of repentance all its days. It will do this by a just and right remembrance of the nature of their sin, its circumstances and aggravations, the shameful unkindness toward God that it showed, the grief of the Holy Spirit, and the dishonor to Christ.

Indeed, where faith does not do this, the sincerity of a person's recovery from great sins should be justly questioned. It is because of a lack of this conviction that so many palliated[1] cures of great sins occur, followed by fearful and dangerous relapses. Consider a man who has been subject to great corruptions and temptations, has been surprised by them into great actual sins, and has seemingly recovered through humiliation and repentance. If he then again breaks the yoke of this repentance, he will again be quickly overcome, perhaps beyond recovery. It is only he who walks softly who walks safely.

2. This special repentance is also necessary for those whose failures have caused scandal and offense. This will stick very close to any who have the least spark of saving faith. These sorts of sins in God's people especially provoke Him, as we see in David's case in 2 Samuel 12:14 (see also Ezek. 36:20; Rom. 2:24). Scandal keeps the remembrance of sin alive and continually sets it before men. In a gracious soul, saving faith is a spring of all acts and duties of repentance. It was so in David all his days and probably in Mary Magdalene also. Any time this happens, faith will keep the soul in a humble and contrite state and watchful against pride, elation of mind, carelessness, and sloth. It will recover godly sorrow and

1. To "palliate" means to lessen the symptoms of a disease without removing its cause.

shame, with self-reflection, in great humbling of mind—all intended in this state of repentance. Anyone who can easily shake off a sense of scandal caused by sin has very little Christian sincerity.

3. This special degree of repentance is also necessary to those who have troubling and entangling lusts and corruptions. Such corruptions join with temptations to frequently disquiet, wound, and defile the soul. This wearies the soul, and it cries for deliverance (Rom. 7:24). When the soul is in this state, faith will spur it to prayer, watchfulness, and diligence in opposition to the deceit and violence of sin. But this is not all. Faith will not rest here, but will give the mind a sense of its distressed and dangerous condition, to fill it constantly with godly sorrow, humiliation, and all duties of repentance. No man can hold out in such a conflict nor maintain his peace on just grounds if he does not live in the constant exercise of repentance. Those who look for victory or peace will be mistaken if they think they may carry on their general way of duties and profession while they have untamable corruptions working in their minds. These sorts of persons are above all others especially called to this state and duty of repentance.

4. The next category are those who mourn for the sins of the place and age in which they live, as they consider the consequences of the dishonor of God and the judgments which will follow because of them. There are times in

which this is a special and honorable duty of which God highly approves. Such times are when the visible church is greatly corrupted and open abominations are among men of all sorts, like it is today. In such times, the Lord declares how much He values the performance of this duty, as He testifies in Ezekiel 9:4. Only those who thus mourn shall be under His special care in a day of public distress and calamity. I'm afraid that this is a duty in which most of us are very defective. We cannot attain the frame of heart required for this nor perform the duty rightly, outside this state of repentance and humiliation that we are examining. Without it we may have fleeting thoughts of these things, but they will only affect our minds very little. But when we keep our souls in this spiritual frame, we will always be ready for this duty.

5. This duty also becomes those who, having passed through the greatest part of their lives, find that the pursuit of worldly things results in vanity, as Solomon wrote in Ecclesiastes. When a man describes the various scenes of his life and the various conditions he has been in, he may possibly find nothing but sorrow and trouble. This may be true even with the good and best of men, as it was with Jacob. Others may have received more satisfaction in the course of their lives, but if they look back, they also find how little satisfaction fleeing comforts bring. They will say, "There is nothing in these things; it is high time to take off all expectations from them." Such

people seem called to this special exercise of repentance and mourning for the remainder of their lives.

6. This duty is necessary for those whose hearts are so wounded and deeply affected by the love of Christ that they can hardly bear any longer absence from Him, nor delight in the things that keep them out of His presence. The apostle describes this condition in 2 Corinthians 5:8: "We are confident, I say, and willing rather to be absent from the body, and to be present with the Lord" (see also vv. 2, 4, 6). They live in a state of groaning, thoroughly aware of all the evils that accompany them in this absence of the Bridegroom. They continually reflect on the sins and follies that have filled (and continue to fill) their lives. Therefore, as their hearts are filled with inflamed affections toward Christ, they must walk humbly and mournfully until they come to Him. Those who have experience of such love for the Lord Jesus cannot help having continual reason for joy in themselves, and so they have the least need of such a state of constant humiliation and repentance. They do have such reasons for joy, and thus Christ will be formed in them more and more every day (Gal. 4:19). But there is no inconsistency between spiritual joy in Christ and godly sorrow for sin. In fact, no man in this life shall ever be able to maintain solid joy in his heart without the continual working of godly sorrow. There is a secret joy and refreshment in godly sorrow, and a great spiritual satisfaction that is equal to our highest joys.

What Duties Are Required in This Special State of Repentance?

Before I show what this state of repentance looks like and what is required for it, we should look at three rules for rightly evaluating ourselves in this duty.

1. Faith will demonstrate its reality in its sincere endeavor after the things intended, even though its accomplishments in some of them are small or weak. Indeed, a sense of one's shortcomings in a full compliance with these things is an important ingredient in this mindset. Therefore, if faith keeps up this goal, sincerely pursuing it even though it may fail or not see any progress, it will show its integrity.

2. There are, as we shall see, several things required in this repentance, but not everyone in this state of repentance possesses them all to the same degree as others may. Some may be more notable in one of them, some in another. Some may make great progress in certain places while some may find great obstacles. But all of these aspects must be rooted in the heart at all times and be put forth in exercise sometimes on their proper occasions.

3. The description of this state of repentance distinguishes it from that discontent of mind because of which some people who are weary from the disappointments of this world withdraw themselves from the occasions

of life and condemn others rather than themselves. This mindset has set some on a crooked path.

The First Requirement: Detachment from the World

The first thing this special repentance requires is being weaned from the world. Most people think that as long as they keep themselves from known particular sins of the world they are acceptable, and they do not care how much they cling to the world. They may be swallowed up with the business and occasions of the world. Some will pretend to have an outwardly strict way of life, while their hearts and affections clearly cling to the things of the world. But the foundation of this work of faith we are examining must be laid in mortification and being weaned from the world.

In ancient times, various people devised a strict manner of mortification and penitence. They always laid the foundation of mortification in a renunciation of the world. But most of them fell into a threefold mistake, which ruined the whole undertaking.

First of all, they neglected natural and moral duties that were indispensably required of them. They forsook their natural responsibilities as fathers, children, husbands, wives, and the like, retreating into solitude. By this they also lost all of the social and Christian usefulness to which we are obligated by the principles of human society and of our religion. They adopted a manner of life that made the most important Christian duties, such as respecting all kinds of people in all fruits of love, utterly impossible. They could no longer be useful or helpful in the places and circumstances in which they had been set by divine providence. They could not expect any blessing from God in this way. But the renunciation of the world that we propose requires no such thing. Christian duties do not interfere with our spiritual lives or make us useless to others. While we are in the world, we are to use the world, but not abuse it. We must still do good to all people, as the opportunity arises. Indeed, no one will be more ready for life's duties than those who are most weaned from the world. Thoughts of retreating from usefulness to others are temptations, unless they are caused by a decrease in physical health and strength.

The second error is that they engaged in practices that Scripture does not require. These included outward manners, fasting, dietary restrictions, and ritual times of prayer, to which they eventually added severity to the body and ascetic practices. This plan resulted in a meticulous, superstitious observance of these things, which gave rise and occasion to innumerable evils. Faith does not direct us to such practices. Faith guides us to no duties but those that are according to the rule of the Word.

The third mistake these persons made is that they eventually engaged themselves by vows to the orders and rules of pretended religious life as were proposed to them by some of their leaders. This ruined the whole plan.

However, their original purpose was good, for they sought to renounce the world in order to keep it and its ways from hindering us from walking humbly before God. We are to be crucified to the world, and the world to us, by the cross of Christ. And if we are motivated by faith, in humiliation and repentance, we are to be weaned from the world in a special manner. This requires five things:

1. First of all, we must mortify our affections for the desirable things of the world. These affections are naturally keen and sharp. They are set on worldly things and cling to them tenaciously, especially when they have a place in our hearts through the nearness of human relationships, such as husbands, wives, children, and so on. People are prone to think that they can never love family members or friends sufficiently and can never do enough for them. I grant that they are to be preferred above all earthly blessings. But when they fill and possess the heart—when they weaken and dull our affections for spiritual, heavenly, and eternal things—then the heart will never be in a good frame or capable of the degree of grace in repentance which we seek. We need to be mortified even to these desirable things of the world. Many think they can never overvalue or cling too closely to these and other useful things in the world, such as outward wealth, prosperity, and peace. But we must begin here if we intend to take one step into this holy

detachment from the world. We must remove the edge of our affections and desires for these things.

There are three things necessary for this:

First, we must have a clear and constant perspective of the uncertainty, emptiness, and inability of worldly things to give us any rest or satisfaction. The Scriptures show the things of the world to be uncertain riches, uncertain enjoyments, things that perish and pass away—indeed, it says they are passing snares, burdens, and obstacles, and so they are. If the mind were continually settled in this opinion of worldly things, it would daily lessen its delight and satisfaction in them.

Second, we must constantly endeavor for conformity to Christ crucified. It is by the cross of Christ that we are crucified unto the world and all things in it (Gal. 6:14). When the mind, if it has any spark of saving faith in it, is consumed with thoughts of Christ, especially the manner and purpose of His death, it will keep the eyes from looking on the desirable things of this world with any delightful, friendly view. The things of the world will seem to the mind dead and discolored.

Third, we must also steadily fix our minds on spiritual and eternal things, which I have written about elsewhere.[2] The apostle gives us the whole of this advice

---

2. See John Owen, *The Grace and Duty of Being Spiritually Minded*, in *The Works of John Owen*, ed. W. H. Goold (Edinburgh: Banner of Truth, 1966), 7:261–497; and Owen, *Meditations and Discourses on the Glory of Christ*, in *Works*, 1:273–417.

in Colossians 3:1–5, where he exhorts us to set our affections on things above.

When these are done, faith begins to work. Self-denial, of which this mortification is a principal part, is the first lesson faith takes from the gospel. In this it labors to cast off every burden and the sin that so easily besets us. All further attempts in this great duty of repentance will be fruitless, unless some progress is made here. Do any of you, then, judge that you, under any of those qualifications before mentioned, are in need of this duty and work of faith? Consider that unless you can remove your hearts from the world; unless your affections and desires are mortified, crucified, and dead in you in a noticeable degree and measure; unless you endeavor every day to take this frame of mind, then you will live and die as strangers to this duty.

2. When we mortify our affections toward these things, our love, desire, and delight will produce a moderation of passions, such as fear, anger, sorrow, and the like. Men are stirred up to these passions in changes, losses, and trials. Such people are prone to be vulnerable in those tempers. They take everything to heart. Every affliction and disappointment is exaggerated, as if no one else experienced these things as they have. Everything puts them into a commotion. So when any upset occurs in their lives, they are surprised with anger about trifles and influenced by fear, along with other turbulent passions. This is why men are morose, peevish, cross, and

prone to be displeased and offended on all occasions. Part of faith's work is subduing this state of mind, casting out these attitudes and sinful inclinations. When the mind is weaned from the world and the things of the world, it will be calm, quiet, composed, and not easily moved by the occurrences and occasions of life. The mind becomes unmoved by these things, and in a great measure unconcerned in them. This is that "moderation" of mind in which the apostle would have us excel (Phil. 4:5). He says it should be so eminent that it will appear unto "all men"; that is, all who know us (relations, family, and other circles). This moderation is what renders us most useful and exemplary in this world. Because they lack it, many professing Christians fill themselves and others with anxiety and give offense to the world itself. God requires all believers to hate the things of the world, but those whom faith weans from its attractions, for this special exercise of repentance, will be especially distinguished in it.

3. Being weaned from the world also requires us to give up anxiety concerning present affairs and future events. Scripture's most strict command is that we should be anxious about nothing and have no anxious thought for tomorrow, but rather commit all things to the sovereign disposal of our God and Father, who has taken all these things into His own care. But through the vanity of men's minds, things which they need not even consider become almost hellish to them. Worry about present

things and anxiety about things to come, either private or public affairs, takes up most of their thoughts and plans. But faith will subdue anxiety when it promotes repentance by detachment from the world. It will bring the soul into a constant, steady, and full resignation of itself to God's pleasure and will. On this basis, the soul will use the world without abusing it, with an absolute lack of anxious concern regarding what may happen. Our Savior presses this upon us at length and provides many divine reasons for doing so in Matthew 6:25–34.

4. Being weaned from the world requires a constant preference for the duties of religion before and above the duties and occasions of life. The duties and occasions of life will continually interfere if we do not keep a diligent watch over them, and they will fight for preference. Their success depends on the interest and esteem that the things themselves hold in our minds. If interest in the world is prevalent in our minds, then we will prefer the occasions of the world to religious duties, and our duties shall, for the most part, be put off until a time in which we have nothing else to do and we are fit for little else. But when the interest of spiritual things prevails in the mind, it will be different, according to the command given us by our blessed Savior: "Seek ye first the kingdom of God, and his righteousness" (Matt. 6:33).

This rule, I confess, is not absolute in all seasons and occasions. There may be a time in which Sabbath observation must allow pulling an ox or donkey out of a pit. On all such occasions the rule is that mercy is to be preferred before sacrifice. But, in our ordinary walk before God, faith will take care that we prefer duties of religion above all the occasions of this life. They shall not be shuffled off by trivial excuses nor put off into untimely seasons. Watching in prayer also belongs to this being weaned from the world, which is necessary for notable growth of humiliation and repentance.

5. Finally, this being weaned from the world requires a willingness and readiness to part with all for Christ and the gospel. This is the animating principle of the great duty of taking up the cross and denying ourselves. We cannot be Christ's disciples without some measure of this sincere willingness. But this special repentance requires a significant degree of this willingness, which Christ calls the *hating* of all things in comparison to Him. Such a readiness rejects with contempt everything that argues against it. It establishes a determined resolution in the mind, so that as God requires, we should forsake the world and all its concerns for Christ and the gospel. Our attitudes and speech in difficulties do not argue that this resolution is prevalent in us—it is required in that work of faith that we are considering.

The Second Requirement: Remembering Our Sins with Self-Loathing

The second thing special repentance requires is a particular remembrance of sin and reflection on it, with self-dissatisfaction and abhorrence. God has promised in His covenant, "Their sins and their iniquities will I remember no more" (Heb. 8:12)—that is, punish them. But it does not follow that *we* should remember them no more, but, instead, we are to bear them in mind and be humbled for them. Repentance always regards sin; wherever, therefore, there is repentance there will be a continual calling sin to remembrance. As the psalmist said, "My sin is ever before me" (Ps. 51:3). There are three ways in which we can call our past sins to remembrance.

The first way is with delight and contentment. Thus is it with debauched sinners, whose bodies can no longer serve their youthful lusts. They call over their former sins, roll them over in their minds, express their delight in them by their words, and hate nothing more than the fact that they cannot still practice them, either because of the lack of strength or opportunity. This is to be old in wickedness and to have their bones filled with the sins of their youth. Many in this age delight in filthy communication, unclean society, and all incentives of lust; this is a fearful sign of being given over to a depraved mind and a heart that cannot repent.

The second remembrance of sin leads to anxiety, terror, and despair. Where men's consciences are not seared with a hot iron, sin will visit their minds now and then with a troublesome memory of an action, with its aggravating circumstances. For the most part, men hide from this visitor. They are not at home, do not have time to speak with it—they put it off, day after day, like penniless debtors, with a few fleeting thoughts and words. But sometimes it cannot be put off. It will come with an arrest or a warrant from God's law that will call them to stand and give an account of themselves. Then they are filled with anxiety, sometimes even with horror and despair, which they seek to pacify and distract themselves from by immersing themselves even deeper in the pursuit of their lusts. See the case of Cain in Genesis 4:13, 16–17.

But the third way we call our sins for remembrance is to help further repentance. In this case the sins act as a triple mirror to the soul.

1. The soul sees in its sins the corruption of its nature—the evil quality of the root that has brought forth such fruit. They see in it their own folly, how they were cheated by sin and Satan. They see the ingratitude and unkindness toward God that accompanied their sins, and this fills them with holy shame (Rom. 6:21). This is useful and necessary to repentance. Perhaps if men thought about their former sins and failures more often than they do, they would walk more humbly and warily than they usually do. So David in his old age prays for a renewed sense of the pardon of the sins of his youth (see Ps. 25:7).

2. The soul sees a representation of the grace, patience, and pardoning mercy of God. "This was my condition. God could have justly cast me away forever. He could

have cut me off in the midst of these sins, without leisure to cry for mercy. Perhaps I continued long in some of these sins. Oh, the infinite patience of God that spared me! The infinite grace and mercy of God, that forgave me for these provoking iniquities!" This is the frame of mind expressed in Psalm 103:2–4: "Bless the LORD, O my soul, and forget not all his benefits: who forgiveth all thine iniquities; who healeth all thy diseases; who redeemeth thy life from destruction; who crowneth thee with lovingkindness and tender mercies."

3. The soul sees in its sins the efficacy of Christ's blood and mediation (1 John 2:2). The soul must ask, "Why do I have deliverance from the guilt of these sins? What way was made for grace to pardon them? Why are my soul and conscience purged from the stain and filth of my sins?" Here the whole glory of the love and grace of Christ in His mediation, with the worth of the atonement He made and the ransom He paid, with the efficacy of His blood to purge us from all our sins, is represented to the mind of the believer. So "out of the eater came forth meat" (Judg. 14:14). By this remembrance of sin, reconciliation is made between the deepest humiliation and a refreshing sense of the love of God and peace with Him.

A soul that is engaged into the paths of repentance will, therefore, constantly apply itself to this remembrance of sin. Faith alone provides this view of redemption in the face of sin. No other light will reveal them in this way—in any other light they are horrid and terrifying and fill the soul with dread and thoughts of fleeing from God. But this view of them is suited to stir up all graces to holy exercise.

The Third Requirement: Godly Sorrow for Sin

Godly sorrow will follow our remembrance of sin, and this sorrow is the very life and soul of repentance. The apostle Paul teaches this in 2 Corinthians 7:9–11.[3] This passage encompasses all that Scripture says about a broken heart and a contrite spirit, which expresses itself by sighs, tears, mourning, and even in watering our beds with tears. David exemplifies this, and his example is so frequently repeated that we need no other illustration. I shall not insist upon it in general but show only two things: what it concerns; and in what it consists—that is, how faith works it in the soul.

1. Godly sorrow is concerned with a twofold object: past sins and daily infirmities. It addresses past sins by reason of their own nature or their aggravations that have

3. "Now I rejoice, not that ye were made sorry, but that ye sorrowed to repentance: for ye were made sorry after a godly manner, that ye might receive damage by us in nothing. For godly sorrow worketh repentance to salvation not to be repented of: but the sorrow of the world worketh death. For behold this selfsame thing, that ye sorrowed after a godly sort, what carefulness it wrought in you, yea, what clearing of yourselves, yea, what indignation, yea, what fear, yea, what vehement desire, yea, what zeal, yea, what revenge! In all things ye have approved yourselves to be clear in this matter."

left the greatest impression on the conscience. Indeed, it recalls, in general, all past and known sins that it can remember. But usually, in the course of men's lives, there have been some sins whose wounds, on various accounts, have been deepest and felt the most. These are the special objects of godly sorrow. So it was with David: in the whole course of his life, after his great fall, he still bewailed his sin; and he did the same for the other sins of his youth. Everyone has something like this that provokes them and that may be a just cause of this sorrow all their days. But in addition to past sins, godly sorrow addresses the daily attacks of infirmities, in failures and negligence in our minds or actions, which even the best believers are subject to. These are a matter of continual sorrow and mourning to a gracious soul that is engaged in this duty and way of repentance.

2. Second, godly sorrow consists in the following things: self-judging, humiliation, anxiety, mourning, and motivation.

Self-judging is the ground and spring of all godly sorrow, and it is followed by repentance. Paul says that it turns away the displeasure of God (1 Cor. 11:31). The soul continually judges itself with reference to the sins previously mentioned. It passes sentence on itself every day. This cannot be done without grief and sorrow, for although the soul finds it a necessary duty and is, on that basis, well pleased with it, all such self-reflections are like afflictions and are not joyful, but full of grief.

Self-reflection results in constant *humiliation*. Whoever judges himself knows what frame of mind and spirit he possesses. This removes the ground of all pride and self-pleasing. Where there is self-judging, these things can have no place. God promises to approve of this frame of mind, and Scripture reveals that the humble are the special object of God's own care. He regards those who are of a broken heart and a contrite spirit. This humility grows on no other root. No man, no matter how diligent on any argument or consideration, can bring himself into that humble frame in which God is delighted unless he lay a foundation of continual self-judging for it. Men may put on a fashion or frame of humility, but they are not really humble. Where man lacks humility, pride is on the throne and in his heart, though he may have a humble countenance or behavior.

In godly sorrow there is real trouble and *anxiety* of mind, for sorrow is an afflictive passion. It is contrary to the composure which the mind would like to maintain. Nevertheless, this trouble is not the kind that is opposed to spiritual peace and refreshment. For it is an effect of faith, and faith will not produce anything that is inconsistent with peace with God or that will challenge it. But this anxiety is opposite to other comforts. It is a trouble that earthly things cannot remedy. The psalmist, on all occasions, expressed the trouble of his mind to God in his sorrow for sin. Sometimes, like throughout Psalm 88, it rises to such a great and dreadful height that he compares himself to a dead man. Sometimes this anxiety overwhelms the soul, but only to find relief by pouring out its complaint before the Lord (Ps. 102:1).

This inward state of trouble, *mourning*, and contrition will express itself on all just occasions by outward signs of sighs, tears, and mournful complaints (Ps. 31:10). David continually mentions his tears. Peter, on review of his sin, wept bitterly (Luke 22:62). Mary washed the feet of Christ with her tears, as we all should. A soul filled with sorrow will overflow and express its inward frame by these outward signs. I speak not of those self-whole, always cheerful professors that abound these days. Whoever faith engages in this duty of sorrow will abound in these outward signs. I fear there is too great a pretense among us that men's natural tempers and attitudes are unyielding and unaffected by these things. Where God makes the heart soft, and godly sorrow not only occasionally visits the heart but dwells in it, such sorrow will not be absent. What it falls short of in one way, it may make up in another. Whatever the case is as to tears, it is certain that sighs and groans for sin are not contrary to any man's nature but only to the sin engrafted in it.

Finally, this godly sorrow will constantly *motivate* the mind toward all duties, acts, and fruits of repentance, whatever they are. It is never barren or heartless. Since it is both a grace and a duty, it will stir up the soul to the exercise of all graces and the performance of all duties. The apostle Paul declares this fully in 2 Corinthians 7:11.

Godly sorrow, therefore, is another requirement that belongs to the state of repentance brought about by faith. Indeed, if this sorrow is constant and effective, it is the clearest evidence of saving faith. Those who mourn for their sin are blessed (Matt. 5:4). I would almost say that this is worth all other evidences, for without godly sorrow, there are none at all. Where this frame is not present, in some good measure, the soul can have no meaningful evidence of its good estate.

The Fourth Requirement: Fitting Outward Action against Sin

The fourth requirement belonging to this state of repentance is taking fitting outward action against sin, such as abstinence, for the genuine mortification of the flesh.[4] I do not mean mortification that is harmful to the body and actually becomes a hindrance to greater duties. Some have made great mistakes in this matter; most men have fallen into extremes about it, as is common. For example, men retained in the papacy, from the beginning of the apostasy of the Roman Church

4. For Owen's fuller treatment of mortification, see *Of the Mortification of Sin in Believers*, in *Works*, 6:1-86; as well as the discussion on mortification in book 4, chapter 8 of *Pneumatologia*, in *Works*, 3:538–65. For a contemporary and more accessible study of mortification, see Brian G. Hedges, *Licensed to Kill: A Field Manual for Mortifying Sin* (Adelphi, Md.: Cruciform Press, 2011).

from the rule of the Scripture, a belief that mortification was necessary for a penitent state. But they mistook the nature of this mortification and instead practiced, for the most part, what Paul calls the "doctrines of devils" when he foretold that hypocritical apostasy (1 Tim. 4:1–3). The substance of their mortification was celibacy (and so they made vows against the use of marriage, which is God's ordinance), and they required abstinence from meats in various laws and rules under pretense of great holiness. They added habits, fasting, disciplines, rough garments, and innumerable, similar ascetic practices. But men have long since detected the vanity of this hypocrisy. On the other hand, most men fall to the other extreme. Men generally judge that they have full liberty in using the things regarded as refreshments of nature. Indeed, they judge that they have free and lawful use of all things, when, in fact, they are under the greatest need for godly sorrow and direct repentance. But this mistake is just as dangerous a mistake as the former. This is what the Lord Jesus Christ charges us to watch against in Luke 21:34–36.

This, therefore, is required for the state of repentance we are considering: things that restrain the satisfaction of the appetite while turning from the joyful enticements of the world, walking heavily and mournfully, and expressing a humble and afflicted spiritual frame. The mourners in Zion are not to be ashamed of their lot and state but are to profess it in suitable outward demonstrations. They are to profess it not in unrestrained habits and gestures, like the monks; and not in dramatic forms of speech and barbaric behavior, like some among ourselves; but in ways that naturally express the inward frame of mind that we are considering.

The Fifth Requirement: A Firm Watchfulness over Times of Solitude

The fifth requirement is a firm watchfulness over times of solitude, both night and day, with a continual readiness to fight temptations at their first appearance in order that they will not surprise the soul.[5] The purpose in the exercise of this grace is to constantly keep and preserve the soul in a humble and contrite frame. If that is lost at any time, the whole design for that period of time is thwarted. Faith, therefore, engages the mind to watch against two things: the times and means by which we may lose this frame.

1. We must watch over our *times* of solitude and retirement, by night or by day, more carefully than any other time. In these times we see what we are—these are either the best or the worst of our times, when the predominant principle in us will show itself. That is why some are said to "devise iniquity, and work evil upon their

---

5. Owen discusses the nature of watchfulness in *Of Temptation*, in *Works*, 6:127–49.

beds! when the morning is light, they practise it" (Mic. 2:1). Their solitude in the night helps them to think on, contrive, and delight in all the iniquity that they intend to accomplish in the day. On the other hand, the work of a grace-filled soul in such times is to seek after Christ (Song 3:1)—to be meditating on God, as the psalmist often puts it. So the humble soul is diligently watchful that at such seasons, vain imaginations, which pry themselves into the mind, do not carry it away and cause it to lose its spiritual frame, even if for a season. Indeed, these are the times that the humble soul seizes for its sanctification. This is when it beckons all those considerations of sin and grace, which help to affect and lower the soul.

2. Temptations are the *means* by which we may lose this humble frame. Temptations strive to possess the mind either by sudden surprises or continuous luring. A soul engaged by faith in the duty of watchfulness is always aware of the deceit and violence of temptations. It knows that if temptations enter the soul, and entangle it, even just for a time, they will quite cast out or deface that humble, contrite, broken frame that the soul seeks to preserve. And anyone who has the least grain of spiritual wisdom understands the kinds of temptations to which he is most vulnerable. Faith sets the soul on its continual watch and guard over these places and makes it ready to combat every temptation on its first appearance. For temptation is then weakest and most

easily subdued. The soul will not allow temptations to gain time, ground, or strength. This is how it preserves a humble frame and often delivers itself from the jaws of this devourer.

The Sixth Requirement: Deep Longing for Deliverance
The sixth requirement in this state of repentance is a deep longing for deliverance. For even though the soul finds satisfaction in keeping this humble frame, though it is never sinfully weary of it, and even labors to grow and thrive in the spirit and power of it, yet it is constantly accompanied with deep sighs and groans for deliverance. These groanings express longing for both deliverance and glory. During the time between conversion and final deliverance, sighs and longings fill the soul.

1. The soul groans for deliverance *from* the remaining power of sin. For it is sin and its remaining power that distress and disturb the soul. Occasionally, the presence of remaining sin increases the soul's humility, mourning, and self-abasement, but this is because of Christ's effectual grace. Sin leads to hurt and ruin. The apostle Paul emphatically expresses this in his own person: "O wretched man that I am! who shall deliver me from the body of this death?" (Rom. 7:24).

This constant groaning for deliverance from the power of sin also rouses the soul to pursue sin's destruction. This is an effect of faith, and no such effect is heartless or fruitless. It will be operative toward what it aims at—in this case the eradication of sin. The soul groans after this. The soul contends for this. This is the work of faith, and "faith without works is dead" (James 2:20). The soul, therefore, continually pursues sin's destruction. Since the soul can have no rest from sin, neither will the soul give rest or peace to sin. Indeed, a constant endeavor to eradicate sin is a blessed evidence of a saving faith.

2. The soul not only groans for deliverance from sin, however; it also groans *for* the full enjoyment of glory (Rom. 8:23). This is the grace and duty of all believers, all who have received the firstfruits of the Spirit. All believers groan, in some measure, that their very bodies may be delivered from being the subject and seat of sin. We long for the perfect deliverance of our bodies from sin, which shall complete the grace of adoption in the whole person. But longing is most prominent in those who are most humble and repentant. They, if any, groan earnestly. They continually sigh, breathe, and pant after this deliverance, and their views of the glory that God will reveal refresh them in their deepest sorrows. They wait for the Lord in this more than they that wait for the morning. Do not blame a truly penitent soul if he longs to be dissolved; the excellence of the change he will have is his present life and relief.

3. But this desire to be dissolved is held in check by the natural desire to continue living. Faith reconciles these

conflicting inclinations, keeping the soul from weariness and impatience. Faith does this by reminding the soul not to be absolutely governed by either of these desires. Faith first keeps these desires from excess by teaching the soul to regulate them both by the Word of God. Faith makes God's Word the rule of such desires and inclinations. As long as God's Word regulates them, they will not offend. Faith also mixes a grace with these desires that makes them useful: constant submission to God's will. "Grace desires to pass away and be with Christ, while nature desires to keep on living," says the soul. "But my rule is the will and sovereign pleasure of God. 'Not my will, holy Father, but Thy will be done.'" Christ Himself is our example of this.

The Seventh Requirement: Abounding in Thoughts of Spiritual Things

The last thing I will mention is abounding in thoughts and meditations of heavenly, invisible, and eternal things. This completes the state of repentance we have described. No one has more holy and humble thoughts than truly penitent souls. No people have more high and heavenly contemplations. You might take them to be all sighs, all mourning, all dejection of spirit, but those who exercise gospel faith through this special repentance are raised higher than any others. They are closer to the high and lofty One who inhabits eternity, for God dwells with them. "For thus saith the high and lofty One that inhabiteth eternity, whose name is Holy;

I dwell in the high and holy place, with him also that is of a contrite and humble spirit, to revive the spirit of the humble, and to revive the heart of the contrite ones" (Isa. 57:15).

As God dwells with believers in this state of repentance, so they dwell with Him in a special manner by these heavenly contemplations. Those who have the lowest thoughts of themselves and are most filled with self-abasement have the clearest views of divine glory. The best view of the stars is from the bottom of a pit. The soul in its deepest humiliations has, for the most part, the clearest views of things within the veil.